Eduardo Milán

Selected Essays

Also by Eduardo Milán from Shearsman Books:

Selected Poems

Eduardo Milán

Selected Essays

Edited by Antonio Ochoa

Introduced by William Rowe

Translated by
Leslie Harkema, Ruth Hemus,
David Nielsen & Antonio Ochoa

Shearsman Books

Published in the United Kingdom in 2016 by
Shearsman Books Ltd
50 Westons Hill Drive
Emersons Green
BRISTOL
BS16 7DF

Shearsman Books Ltd Registered Office
30-31 St. James Place, Mangotsfield, Bristol BS16 9JB
(this address not for correspondence)

www.shearsman.com

ISBN 978-1-84861-474-1

Copyright © Eduardo Milán, 2016.
Selection copyright © Antonio Ochoa, 2016.
Introduction copyright © William Rowe, 2016.
Translations copyright © Leslie Harkema,
Ruth Hemus, David Nielsen and Antonio Ochoa, 2016.

The right of Eduardo Milán to be identified as the author of this work has been asserted by him in accordance with the Copyrights, Designs and Patents Act of 1988.
All rights reserved.

Contents

William Rowe
Introduction: Writing Without Alibis:
   The Essays of Eduardo Milán   7

1.
Premise   15
Talking about Parra   18
A Brazilian Odysseus :
   The Poetry of Haroldo de Campos   31
The Present of Martínez Rivas   41

2.
An Essay on Poetry   51
Parra and Concrete Poetry   75

3.
To Write About Writing Poetry   85
Key Words:
   A Few Words to Defend, Not Everything
      Can Be Negotiated   88

Between Listeners, Loss :
   A Conversation with Eduardo Milán   97

Writing Without Alibis:
The Essays of Eduardo Milán

William Rowe

The temptation of myth, the temptation of pity, and the temptation of culture: these lie in wait for the essayist and by the same token are means by which the literary essayist defines his/her present. Though all three seek to elude the writer's consciousness, the first two have a known face. The temptation of myth was exposed by the historical avant-gardes: Milán mentions among others T.S. Eliot, whose poem 'The Waste Land' reveals 'the emptying of the symbolic universe' which occurs in the contemporary world. As for the temptation of pity, which has to do with history, i.e., with the human atrocities of the twentieth century, there is the work of César Vallejo, or of Raúl Zurita, with their sense that what is at stake is not relief from horror but attainment of messianic redemption ('to kill death', in Vallejo's phrase). But the temptation of symbolic capital, which is now called culture, is less easy to expose. There is also the temptation of philosophy, i.e., of the theorization of literature, but that has been overtaken in the last decade or two by the lure of cultural capital. Although Pierre Bourdieu can be credited with the extension of the term, capital, to the realm of the symbolic economy, he does not provide a critique of the effect he is describing only of its uneven distribution. This is where Guy Debord's notion of the spectacle becomes necessary, as something whose function is to bury history in culture. The spectacle, moreover, looks back at us, constitutes the collective subject, the one whose function it is to consume its own alienation from history.

It is the desire of the poetic word, Milán writes, to 'differentiate itself from its own myth'. Here a whole narrative—in fact the dominant one—of Latin American poetry falls. From Octavio Paz to Eugenio Montejo and others, it is the territory of myth, its promise of the overcoming of time, failed or not, since what is at issue is the territory not the outcome, this is what has dominated statements about poetry, whether in literary essays or in poetry's own comments about itself, its metalanguage. But poetic language, Milán makes it quite clear, can no longer rest within the myth of poetry: a different necessity presses upon it, producing 'the desire to locate itself inside appearance, desire to belong to time and its flow, to define itself concretely in a historical space.' This is the place from which Milán writes, both as poet and as essayist.

But not in order to suppress the desire of the full—timeless, infinite—word, in the name of some post-modernist vision where poetic forms, emptied of their relationship not only with transcendence but also with history, are recycled indiscriminately in a type of low-level parody. Instead, the essays traverse the terrain of Latin American poetry with the urgency of finding not a canon but those moments where its energies, like Walter Benjamin's 'dialectical image', break into the present. In order to do this, they continually interrogate the writing itself, its possibilities and its limits, so that there is always an outside to the poem, i.e., history, but also an inside, the real possibilities of poetic language. Thus, in order to accede to the full meaning of Viel Temperley's *Hospital Británico*, there is the need to have traversed Benjamin's commentary on Paul Klee's painting 'Angelus Novus', where the angel seems, as he gazes at the past, 'as though he is about to move away from something he is fixedly contemplating... he sees one single catastrophe which keeps piling wreckage upon wreckage.' Milán comments that 'in the face of this there is little the poetic word can do in terms of the activation of memory.' By the mid-twentieth century, the relationship between poetic language and the hope of social transformation had become impossible to sustain. But here Milán refuses to abandon the terrain: the poem still is a capability of language not to be found elsewhere and not simply the empty shell of what was once a sacred place now become simply cultural capital. Thus for him poetry is not words to fill an inherited space—marked out by recognizable forms (rhetoric, metaphors, rhythms, typography, etc.)—but the poetic word that must arise out of an interiority, an inner life, and then create, as it becomes externalized into the poem, the form it needs.

The gaze of the angel, who cannot turn away from the image of historical catastrophe (the image is dialectical, since the angel is also held by 'a storm… blowing from paradise'), is supplemented, in Milán's essays, by another gaze, this time mythological: that of Orpheus, who turns back, an act of disobedience to the gods, because he does not want to lose his wife, and in so doing loses her. This makes song itself 'a lost "place"', Milán writes: 'the mythopoetic substance was not 'filled' by the unfolding of history, nor even by the rationalist negation of myth as a whole.' The place remains: historical reason has not been able to fill it. The movement from myth to desire to the unformed present is a recurrent one for Milán. Hence his interest in Lezama Lima, whose writing embodies a fascination with how the invisible, the unknown, becomes image, something that cannot be known in advance and emerges only in the image itself.

Thus poetic writing is never complete, always 'faltada', as Milán puts it, always missing or lacking, making but also unmaking. And unformed or invisible—or pre-ontological—does not mean immaterial: 'the lack (*falta*) in modern poetic writing is not an ethical lack, it is a material lack, it materiality lacking in its sense.' Here, in this core statement, the essays fulfil Ezra Pound's definition of seriousness: a man standing by his own word. Milán stands by his own poetic practice. This, which is shown in his poems, is stated briefly in the essays as a poetics of the signifier, i.e., 'texts which unfold through the phonic contagion of words,' whose genealogy includes Guillaume de Poitiers and Góngora, as well as the twentieth-century avant-gardes (Oliverio Girondo, Haroldo de Campos, etc.). A phonic materiality which becomes a material 'degree zero' and can become itself the te of the poem. Phonic drift or *derive* which is also a drive or pulse so that desire remains and is not captured by the spectacle ('La Libido/ marcha sobre la tierra bella y desconsiderada,' to quote Rodolfo Hinostroza). The materiality of phonic drift escapes the symbolic economy, which would have words consumed and their material disappear or be ejected as a useless residue, and which under globalized neo-liberalism now penetrates into everything—international English turning the tongue of Joyce into a spectacular disease.

Once the poet is left with the spoken language as 'the only material available for making poetry,' other consequences follow. Among them 'the mythology of the poet as an exceptional being... The mythical place granted to the poet by the Western tradition, a tradition that stretches... from classical antiquity to the avant-gardes of the twentieth century.' Thus a moment, that of Nicanor Parra in the nineteen-fifties, delineates a condition of the now, where the necessity—the drive—is to show its constitutive moments. Hence the need to go back through another moment, 1897, the year of the publication of Mallarmé's *Un coup de dés*, in order to locate the present, to say what it is: 'what has failed... that 'shipwreck' that the text insists on, is the ordering of rhetoric and of the network of symbols, the poetic 'enterprise' undertaken from ancient times, immemorially.' So that what Milán gives us is a temporalization of poetry, an account of where it has got to in terms of its own possibilities. There are only two options: either to return to a place of anteriority, before any utterance, and re-enter the word from there, or find the possibility of poetry within the spoken language. What we are given is neither a genealogy of poetry as such, excluding history, nor a 'history of poetry' (subordinating it to a historicist temporality), but the relation of poetry to its outside, where the outside is constituted by poetic language itself. Actually stating what is the inheritance the contemporary poet must abandon, makes it impossible to turn back—except to see the loss—and thus there can be no alibis: 'poetic modernity and its inheritance allow no halfway houses.' After Parra there's 'no mythology except everyday experience'. But that does not mean denying the past, for the sake of a linear idea of development. The past is present in its transformation. That which fails is not lost; the commodity, fathered by capital, is, as Benjamin puts it, 'failed material'; symbolic capital is work that has become dead; the Mallarméan desire remains, 'to give a purer sense to the words of the tribe'; what has changed is that the words are others.

The alibis are those of the poetic establishments that want to inherit cultural capital. For example, there's their interest in a language which speaks as if for the first time, invoking a 'utopia of speech', but which actually means erasing the traces of history from the word: trading in the mythical inheritance of poetry, as if Mallarmé, Parra, Vallejo, Girondo, had never existed. Or there's their promotion of 'conversational' poetry, as if the work of Parra were not a critique of conversation. Not to subordinate poetry to any programme of ideas, to speak of its real possibilities, yet without returning to the past—whether in the shape of the autonomy of poetry as conceived by romanticism, or the transcendence of poetry identified with myth, or the simple identity of aesthetic and social revolutions—this is the difficult task that Milán sets himself.

1

Premise

We do not know if Orpheus really existed. Yet a gesture from his legend, the gaze of Orpheus or Eurydice's disappearance, is to us more poetically electrifying and tragic than the particular details constructed around his possible existence. That moment, that passionate synecdoche where Blanchot situates the beginning of writing ('writing begins with the gaze of Orpheus'), is a splitting that acquires such mythical transcendence that it is capable of configuring the legend and inventing the biography of its hero.

Orpheus' gaze is a ritual gaze, like a myth in itself where the disappearance of what is loved becomes an essential condition for the birth of song. But it is not a myth in itself, the gaze that turns and disappears what was coming behind is the configuration of a literary space. With a turn on its axis, the gaze allows writing to begin. In opposite direction to the gaze, *immediately after*, the song begins to flow. The literary was not created by the myth, and it wasn't a continuation as a different form of the tale: the literary broke off from the myth. The temptation is to break the diachrony of the tale of Orpheus's possible existence and to see in Eurydice's disappearance the beauty of the singer's song, its power, and its mystery. But such a temptation is not real. Eurydice does not transmit energy to Orpheus as something that transmits energy from one pole to another. Orpheus was already singing before Eurydice disappeared. Blanchot accurately places the appearance of writing on the gaze that prompts disappearance, not on the interchange of powers. Not as if Eurydice, in her disappearance, impregnated Orpheus or his song with disappearance. Nevertheless, there is an impregnation of disappearance in writing in our modern and contemporary readings. There is a reading that overflows with disappearance. In the myth of the singer by antonomasia—Orpheus—there is a key situation: the hero's responsibility for the disappearance of the beloved. There is, perhaps, a wanting to know, an impatience, a stupidity—which is to say, a humanity—that informs the hero of loss, that makes him lose, and that loses him.

Is it not our need for tragedy that which reads in the situation a moment that is key yet normal and transforms it into a foundational event? We practice a cultural extraction; we absorb the extract of what is foundational for our culture, not for the myth. Loss and song, loss and writing are transcendent meanings for us, not for the myth. Among other functions that he performs, Orpheus is an agent of civilization, a transformer, a hero. Or is the episode of Eurydice's disappearance the core of tension that makes Orpheus's life's task educational? Orpheus is a wise character. To sing is to know. Above all the song that transforms nature is a song that belongs to the order of Apollo. Singing is beautiful for the Greeks. Beauty is action. That recklessness, that going against the grain of revelation, that hiding produced by recklessness or passion—that by which we get lost—creates rituals, orders, sects, 'mysteries'. But this is an extrapolation, outside the context of a reading that cannot be understood if it is not seen as the internal tension of a tale about an experience. Still, ever since its classical ascendance that inexplicable tension creates the hidden speech of Western poetry, the unsaid that is said because it is contained in what is said. It is an absence added to presence, not by subterfuge but by pregnancy of meaning, by radiance of meaning, and for us, by a need of completeness. I insist: the disappearance of Eurydice is a meaningful event but it is only part of the tale, a part that for us, as Western debtors to the tragedy, has completely impregnated song with meaning. In this disappearance that song suffers—in this operation Orpheus is the song—there is a model of need, as if the myth prefigured its own absence. What is absent—Eurydice—is converted in song as insufficiency and corresponds to a possible future absence of the myth itself. In other words, what went missing went missing because it had to happen, it was over-determined, or determined from above, we would like to say. And so Orpheus is a puppet of the gods, singing is also a foreseeable insufficiency, and so is beauty. Then the myth can indeed be understood as a setback, even that which is contained within the myth as an internal meta-language that would inform us, from its bowels, about the true dimension of beauty. Beauty is an absence and it is what is absent, it is what we have a right to and what is constantly being subtracted from us. But it is also what is absent for order—a cosmos—to be complete. Beauty sacrificed in the name of equilibrium. And also love, which is 'madness'. Yet what is important is the instrument that generates the absence: the gaze. We must keep an eye on this: it is not blindness, which also has had its cultural prestige throughout time, that foretells what shall come, away from the world of things that clutter our sight. It is the gaze.

Translated by Antonio Ochoa

Talking about Parra

The poetry of Nicanor Parra represents a diving into the limits of the possibilities of poetic language. To cast a doubt on those possibilities is not a denial of poetry or of the inherited poetic tradition: it is, precisely, a bringing up to date of the real possibilities of poetic speech. If what reaches the poet is a worn-out tradition accepted as canon but that can no longer withstand usage (not a useless tradition, nor wrongly proposed—erroneous—but worn-out, which can't operate in aesthetic-communicative terms), the poet can, as a privileged exponent of the consciousness of language, depurate or weed-out the land of language. Mallarmé would say 'to purify', granting secular status to the exercise of linguistic cleansing of a once sacred terrain: that of speech. Parra will work by proposing extreme linguistic situations. In order for this exercise not to become a circumlocution, or a self-centered monologue, the poet must establish a contact with the reader. 'Spoken language', the language where the poetry of Parra is inscribed, is also 'heard language'; spoken by the other. The poetic listener actively participates in Parra's poems because he must, insofar as his acceptance of the game and his possibilities for understanding, be aware of the poet's 'linguistic investigations'. This active reader has to assume a distant attitude towards the language that he himself speaks and which he considers 'natural'. He must alienate himself from his own language. In an unfolding effect sought by the texts, this becomes equal to considering language as a material or field to be explored. This is a situation that turns us, or that returns us, to a conception of modern poetry as either a work that consists of a creation that reflects upon the materiality of language or as one that handles a material foreign to ourselves. This code of alienation is ultimately double, that is, alienation from the world and alienation from the subject himself. This defines post-Enlightenment poetry and dominates the ample space of two centuries. However, that alienation used to find comfort precisely in the territory of *poetic* speech, and trusted it as a point of reference and as a favorable space. The great poetry of the nineteenth century fled towards itself; and, sometimes, silencing itself, it literally fled to different geographies as in the often cited case of Rimbaud. With that radicalism now shifted towards spoken language, Parra demands that his reader too 'vacates' his own language, that he distrusts that language, and that he longs for it not nostalgically but critically. If as William Rowe says, for Parra poetry is what has been inherited from Romanticism and Symbolism, and anti-poetry what belongs to the heritage of speech—as if speech constituted its own movement—it would be appropriate to make a couple of clarifications that will locate more accurately the significance of this poetics.[1] (1) For Romantic and Symbolist poetry, poetic language—with exceptions—is located in the antipodes of spoken language. (2) In that inherited poetry there is a rhetorical coding specific to poetic language and consequently unavoidable: (a) it is a language that speaks of the uncommon, of the *other*, of what is absent from spoken language; (b) it is a language that will try to avoid what comes from common speech because it considers that that belongs to the non-poetic by definition; c) poetic language can be sung or said (prioritizing this 'saying' as an act of exclusive language that belongs to a special registry, an *auric* one) but it cannot be *spoken* in the sense of conversing. This presupposes an emitter versed in this special language and estranged from common speech. However, not estranged in the sense of alienated; rather, estranged because he dominates the 'truth' of language. The *reality* of language in the sense that it had for the German Romantics and particularly for Hölderlin: poetry is what is real.[2] This essential and totalizing conception must be understood as prior to language itself, and not created by men in their everyday communications; that is, in conversation. The

---

[1] William Rowe, *Hacia una poética radical* (Rosario: Beatriz Viterbo, Mosca Azul, 1996), pp. 145-171.
[2] Miguel Casado, *De caminar sobre el hielo* (Madrid: Antonio Machado, 2001), pp. 19-23.

Romantic and Symbolist traditions charged the weight of the poetic reality effect either on syntax or the image. It was about creating exceptional levels of perception and transmission. The linguistic surprise was supported by the discovery—unveiling, in fact—of the unusual that dwells in reality, of the infrequent. Taken as categories of being of the Real hidden by everyday life they will give—although only approximately—a true account of the essentiality of the poetic. The poetic, then, appears as a manifest anteriority, as something situated before language. This is what, with extreme lucidity and extraordinary profundity, José Angel Valente called *antepalabra*.[3]

Facing a poetic tradition—the Western tradition—that appears either as worn-out or inoperable in the present, there doesn't seem to be many possibilities for searching: either a return to a position of anteriority, 'before speech', with the supposed creation *ex-nihilo* that such a gesture of anteriority to any 'original saying' presupposes, even though such a return would be virtual or simulated; or a search in the framework of spoken language, which has been largely forgotten when the poetic capability to operate has been challenged.[4] Poetic modernity and its legacy do not admit half measures. Parra knows this, and he opts for the second choice.

If by Enlightenment is understood schematically 'a rationality advocated to the collective interest against the messianic unreason of the poet as hero,'[5] then to have relegated to a second stage the examination of the effects of speech in poetry represents a flagrant contradiction to its principles and its conquest of the autonomy of art. The collective interest should run through the collective language, through which the collective speaks. Although there might be some insight in bequeathing poetic-linguistic examinations to the poets themselves since this is a defined, self-sustained area of not easy access to the uninitiated.

---

[3] José Manuel Cuesta Abad, *Poema y Enigma* (Madrid: Huerga y Fierro, 1999), pp. 307-332. ['Antepalabra' is coined with the prefix from the Latin, 'ante': before; preceding (oed), and 'palabra' word. t. n.]

[4] José Manuel Cuesta Abad, *Poema y Enigma*, pp. 307-332.

[5] Miguel Casado, *De caminar sobre el hielo*, p. 30.

A division of territories takes place here. Novalis's interest in science and Hölderlin's in philosophy and history are struggles not to reduce the effect of the poetic space, but rather to amplify it to the domain of the human sciences. Yet these are exceptions of Romanticism, at least in Germany. The poetic tradition of the Enlightenment will work with the rhetorical opposition of poetic/common language, as in the case of neo-symbolist French poet Jules Laforgue. Laforgue in an attitude of defiance disregarded the rhetorical apparatus of the inherited tradition of Romanticism. His influence was indelible on twentieth century poets within the Anglo-Saxon tradition and language that in the twentieth century would incorporate with special conviction everyday speech into poetry. Ezra Pound acknowledges as much in Canto CXVI, one of the last *Cantos*: 'And I have learned the most from Jules (Jules Laforgue...)'. However, even with Laforgue's exceptional example we still are in the presence of a confrontation with a tradition regarded as a received 'apparatus'; i.e., in the presence of a recognition. In Parra's case, with the exception of the first texts that form *Poemas y antipoemas* [*Poems and anti-poems*] (1954) where in the parodic use of quotations and motifs the legacy is still palpable, tradition is thrown overboard, and thus, from that moment on, running the imminent risk of a shipwreck. The poet keeps spoken language as the sole material available from where to extract poetry. In order for this to be possible, the laying out of a series of premises becomes necessary.

1. Spoken language is the product of the common man

The concept of 'the common man' is assimilated into that of the 'man of the street'; the 'man without (exceptional) qualities'; the man who suffers, who works for a living, who gets lost in the crowd or in himself—the latter with less frequency now—the man who dies like every man without aspirations of transcendence. In the speaker's situation that Parra proposes in his texts, the whole mythology of the poet as an exceptional being provided with psychic-emotional and perceptive attributes that distinguish him from the man of the masses crumbles down. The mythical place given to the poet by the Western poetic tradition breaks down. This tradition drags itself, with moments of more or less intensity, with more or less critical consciousness, from Classical antiquity to the aesthetic-historical avant-garde movements of the twentieth century.

An aside (1897)

This is the year that Mallarmé publishes *Un coup de dés*. This poem signals the closure not only of the problematic period in the wake of enlightened reason and its proclamation for the autonomy of art—Romanticism as reaction, Symbolism as a critique and unveiling of the socio-symbolic roots of the historical purpose of the poem—but a closure as well of the discussion about the statutes given to the poem by Western tradition. Depending on how it is viewed, *Un coup de dés* is a closure but also as an opening of new poetic possibilities. It challenged the ontological statute of the poem from its most immediate perceptive aspect: its facade. The disintegration of the external form of the poem—although with sights to transform that exteriority into the representation of a real identity, a constellation—corresponds to an internal crisis of poetic speech. If it is common in poetry to treat meaning as an assemblage that does not admit separations—expression must correspond to what is expressed and not only be one of the possibilities of articulation—then, as a particularly pronounced characteristic of Mallarmé's poem, expression is deliberately disintegrated, it follows a course, it proposes an image. What is expressed, on the other hand, follows a different course, that of the tradition it pretends to question. Even though it is a poem that anticipates the possibilities of a new form, the language of *Un coup de dés* does not cease to be one more manifestation of Symbolist aesthetics. One in which the linguistic configuration reaches one of its highest peaks. The criticism of the poem is not directed to what is said but to the design of what is said. Poetic language as rhetoric, lexicon, mythology, is not in question. The question encompasses the form of what is articulated. What has failed, not there but in the entire poetic venture, that 'shipwreck' insisted upon in the poem, is the ordering of the rhetorical and the symbolic framework; the poetic 'enterprise' undertaken since times immemorial. In the same way in which the poetic system where the poem is sustained is not affected, neither is the poetic speaker. The poetic speaker remains in his place, in that mythical privileged place granted to him since Orpheus, or before. Mallarmé does not attempt a criticism of the speaker's position or place. There is an ellipsis of the poetic self considered as the ordering force of the text—there is 'someone' who throws the dice, god or 'immemorial demon', yet always from 'eternal circumstances', i.e., since the beginning and for all time. This could presuppose a neutral manipulator of the words; or, simply, a non-speaker, a privileged act in itself as action, an act without agent, the happening of a first creation without owner, as if 'in the beginning' (*in-illo tempore*) there had been the creation but not the creator. This position configures a totalizing conception of the poetic act: it is a complete metaphor. In any case, there is no possibility for an active subject in that creation, and even less for an active subject considered as a common individual. This undertaking is not common, it remains at a safe distance from the common: it happens in *another* place; in, precisely, the *poetic* place.

2. There is no more mythology than everyday experience

The exceptionality of what is lived comes from our everyday experiences, and regarding the transcendence of the subject there is no possible mythical deliverance. For Parra, the speaker cannot find refuge in an imaginary realm that one day will or will not find transformation into the real. For Parra the imaginary is imaginary. I'll quote one of his major poems entitled 'The Imaginary Man':

El hombre imaginario
vive en una mansión imaginaria
rodeada de árboles imaginarios
a la orilla de un río imaginario

De los muros que son imaginarios
penden antiguos cuadros imaginarios
irreparables grietas imaginarias
que representan hechos imaginarios
ocurridos en mundos imaginarios
en lugares y tiempos imaginarios

Todas las tardes tardes imaginarias
sube las escaleras imaginarias
y se asoma al balcón imaginario
a mirar el paisaje imaginario
que consiste en un valle imaginario
circundado de cerros imaginarios

Sombras imaginarias
vienen por el camino imaginario
entonando canciones imaginarias
a la muerte del sol imaginario

Y en las noches de luna imaginaria
sueña con la mujer imaginaria
que le brindó su amor imaginario
vuelve a sentir ese mismo dolor
ese mismo placer imaginario
y vuelve a palpitar
el corazón del hombre imaginario.[6]

[The imaginary man
Lives in an imaginary mansion
Surrounded by imaginary trees

---

[6] Nicanor Parra, *Hojas de Parra* (Santiago de Chile: Ganímedes, 1985), pp. 101-102.

At the edge of an imaginary river
From the imaginary walls
Hang ancient imaginary paintings
Irreparable imaginary cracks
That represent imaginary facts
That happened in imaginary worlds
In imaginary times and places

Every afternoon imaginary afternoon
He climbs imaginary steps
And peeks out the imaginary balcony

At the imaginary landscape
Which consists of an imaginary valley
Circumscribed by imaginary hills

Imaginary shadows
Advance by the imaginary path
Chanting imaginary songs
To the death of the imaginary sun

And in the nights of the imaginary moon
He dreams of an imaginary woman
Who gave him her imaginary love
He feels again that same pain
That same imaginary pleasure
And it palpitates again
The heart of the imaginary man.]

The imaginary as an attribute of consolation in the face of an overwhelming reality ends up circumscribing it. The imaginary fences off reality by means of repetition thus achieving its transubstantiation. The text produces a commotion that resides in the insistence of a language that, at will, overcomes a limiting referential. And it also suggests a contradiction: that the imaginary instance can only be possible in the punctual, obsessive recognition of its condition. This is not about developing the imaginary in the totality of a poetic conception but about the imaginary becoming a theme: not an unfolding but rather a concentration. It is for Parra an explicit recognition that the imaginary already has an enclosure limited to the poem. We find there too the proposal of a disjunction: either everything is real or everything is imaginary. It is, finally, conversational language, narrative conversational language, which accommodates its own logic to underline time after time *the imaginary condition of the imaginary*. That the condition of a man condemned to imagining supposes his liberation, even if momentary, is another song that Parra knows well.

For now, there is neither a mythical place to return to nor a utopia that could exist. Reality, this reality, the one lived by men socially, is the only one there is. The mythical space has either been blocked, and it no longer operates—mythical space considered as an original space, a space to return to—or it has been substituted by new mythological narratives formulated by social and historical needs. The inner-world, the last remaining bastion of resistance against the process that turns man into a thing, is not an alternative for Parra: this is already the place where the spirit gets confused or it confuses us: 'and poetry resides in things or it simply is a mirage of the spirit', he says in 'Los vicios del mundo moderno' [The vices of the modern world].[7] The poetic territory remains the ample, contradictory, discredited yet surprising territory of speech, 'the millenary contribution of all mistakes', as the Brazilian poet Oswald de Andrade calls it.[8] This is the only language that translates our immediate experience, the only one that 'speaks it'. Parra plays constantly with a notion that belongs more to fiction than to poetry and which he handles almost as a necessary condition of his texts: verisimilitude. Verisimilitude not so much of experiences—Parra's speaker/character may live in extraordinary circumstances, even though most of the time they are banal situations converted into extraordinary ones—but

---

[7] Nicanor Parra, *Obra gruesa* (Santiago de Chile: Andrés Bello, 1983), p. 46.
[8] Oswald de Andrade, 'Manifesto de la poesía Pau Brasil', in Jorge Schwartz *Las vanguardias latinoamericanas* (Mexico: Fondo de Cultura Económica, 2002), p. 168.

of the language that manifests them. The language in the poems of Parra must be credible to any man of average intelligence. The need for verisimilitude is a condition for the challenge to the inherited poetic language. In reference to our ancestral poets, a fragment of 'Manifesto' reads:

> Aceptamos que fueron comunistas
> Pero la poesía fue un desastre
> Surrealismo de segunda mano,
> Decadentismo de tercera mano,
> Tablas viejas devueltas por el mar.[9]

> [We accept that they were communists
> But the poetry was a disaster
> Second hand surrealism,
> Third hand decadence,
> Old boards brought back by the sea.]

Does the conceptual disaster that turns into an actual shipwreck alludes to Mallarmé? The verisimilitude of what is said takes the *other* directly into account, without whom the poem cannot complete its circuit, the common *other* not taken into account by traditional poetry: the reader. And when he has explicitly been taken into account, as in the emblematic verse by Baudelaire, 'Hypocrite lecteur—mon semblable—mon frère!,' written at the threshold of *The Flowers of Evil*, he has been marked as an endorsement of the non-operability of the poetic ritual, certifying a complicity in the misunderstanding. Without Baudelaire's evident nostalgia for those times of communion, Parra grants the reader the place he deserves so that poetry does not become again a kind of 'exterior monologue'. This is not, obviously, a consideration out of guilt, nor a concession nor blackmail. Clearly, this is about the reader as receiver of the poem, yet it is also about, particularly, the reader as social companion involved, as the poet himself, in the same thicket of conventions that social life turns out to be. Even further, it is

---

[9] Nicanor Parra, *Obra gruesa*, p. 153.

about the reader as incarnation of the community, an emerging agent in a community for which poetry is necessary, whether or not it recognizes this fact. It is here that William Rowe's brilliant consideration appears: Parra's poems are an invitation to the outside of the text, to the space of the world, to that which is not the poem.[10] Parra's proposal appears as the reverse of the traditional poem that plays its strength in making the reader go *inside* the text. We see again here the crumbling of the privileged standing of the poem as a place of great promises, of gratifications for the spirit, transcendent and still auric; a space where the imaginary freely circulates, yet also an exclusive space, if not completely closed; a space of possible infinity but where the social world enters only codified, purified.

The poetry of the last century, especially that conceived since the historical avant-garde movements, centred its strength in abolishing the difference between the aesthetic—inside—and the vital—outside—worlds. The Mallarméan premise about the 'purification' of the 'words of the tribe' is a signal for more than a simple recognition of the aesthetic necessity of the times. It signals a task, the task assigned to the poet of any historical time. It begins with the conviction that words are contaminated, turned into instruments by the society that employs them as mere communicative means. The poetic word would be the one that breaks free from that situation and recovers its original meaning. The poetic venture would consist in giving back to the word something similar to a *saying of the beginning*, original insofar as near the origin of man. Here a speech as if 'for the first time' would be the utopia of speech, yet not 'for the first time' historically, as this would imply an unfathomable retreat—rather a significant 'for the first time'. We enter here into the dangerous terrain of imaginary speculation, that of religion or, at least, of a trans-historical consideration of the word. Nothing is farther away from Parra's proposal. For Parra the word is a social element extremely meaningful as a historical mark, one that indicates the state of things in the world. It is only this

---

[10] William Rowe, *Hacia una poética radical*, pp. 145-171.

defining temporality of the poetic word that can explain Parra's masterwork about the reception of the text that, in a self-parody, reads in 'Advertencia al lector' [A Warning to the Reader]:

Según los doctores de la ley este libro no debería publicarse:
La palabra arco iris no aparece en él en ninguna parte,
Menos aún la palabra dolor,
La palabra Torcuato.
Sillas y mesas sí que aparecen a granel,
¡Ataúdes! ¡Útiles de escritorio!
Lo que me llena de orgullo
Porque, a mi modo de ver, el cielo se está cayendo a pedazos.[11]

[According to doctors in law this book should not be published:
The word rainbow does not appear anywhere in it,
Even less the word pain,
The word Torcuato.
Chairs and tables do appear in bulks,
Coffins! Desktop utensils!
Which fills me with pride
Because, to my way of seeing things, heaven is falling apart.]

In this case the *outside* of the poem is identified with literary criticism or with what it pretends, in general, to impose: the power of legitimization or disqualification of a work. This criticism of criticism is centred on the lexicon, the space where poetry—or certain poetry, one affiliated with an auric conception of poetic speech—circumscribes its field of action with particular intensity. 'Rainbow' and 'pain', according to this parodic logic, both belong to an aesthetics of dusk ruled by sentimentality. The neo-Romantic affiliation that Parra attributes to them is very clear. But 'Torcuato' is an impossible word for any aesthetic: thus it becomes an emblem or talisman of impossible words in poetry. Impossible, that is, for neoclassic or neo-Romantic aesthetics, though not for an antipoetic aesthetic that takes into account,

---

[11] Nicanor Parra, *Obra gruesa* (Santiago de Chile: Andrés Bello, 1983), p. 26.

in its strategic-provocative display, the constant unveiling of the linguistic absurd. Parra situates himself as receiver of his own work, and assumes the consequences. He marks the limits of any speech, whether poetic or antipoetic. 'Torcuato', more than a proper name, is a word that is not found in the universe of spoken language. Throughout this poem, we see the poet as critic of his own proposal. His criticism is deferred, he makes the reader speak, the specialist ('doctors in law'), and the common person who would expect poetry's linguistic exclusivity, which is what is confronted by Parra. Such exclusivity in 1954, in Chile, and in the rest of Latin America, was translated to the identification of poetry with metaphor. The master of that identification was Pablo Neruda.

One last aside

'Donner en sens plus pur aux mots de la tribu' [to give a purer sense to the words of the tribe] is an often quoted expression of Mallarmé. This is the dilemma: is it not Parra's proposal to place the accent on 'the words of the tribe', disregarding 'to give', 'sense', and 'pure'? If we take Mallarmé's sentence as emblematic of the poet's work, we notice that the charge in the words has changed: 'to give', 'sense', 'pure' are no longer the important elements. By inverse order to their appearance in the sentence, the importance falls now on 'the words of the tribe', from end to beginning. Only by truly acknowledging the situation of the words of the tribe will we give back sense and purity to them. As José Manuel Cuesta Abad points out, 'the giving does not come from outside of language: it is in it';[12] and sense and purity as well.

Translated by Antonio Ochoa

---

[12] José Manuel Cuesta Abad, *Poema y Enigma*, pp. 307-332.

A Brazilian Odysseus :
The Poetry of Haroldo De Campos

To Roberto Appratto

1. It was Haroldo de Campos, the poet and thinker, who managed to keep the spirit of the avant-garde alive in Latin America throughout the entire second half of the twentieth century. Together with his brother Augusto de Campos and Décio Pignatari he founded the concrete poetry movement—considered to be 'the last avant-garde' movement—in Brazil at the beginning of the 1950s. This point in his production and in his thinking represents a key moment, a matrix even, that has left an indelible mark on contemporary Brazilian poetry and, to a large extent, on Latin American poetry. It was a crucial moment as much for our poetry in general as for his own individual concept of creation. It was 'the grain of sand that protects from tedium', a touchstone, an illumination of Latin American poetry that, like it or not, divided the waters of creative language in two: on the one hand, poetry based on rigour and, on the other, (self) complacent poetry. Such a parting of the poetic waters was the result of a 'foreign body' surging onto the poetry scene that considered poetry to be a lucid and critical activity, made no concessions, and paid it its due homage. Elsewhere, I've talked about the formal conditions of the concrete poem, its constructive consciousness, the opposition that it represents to the traditional conception of the poem, the historical models to which it appeals, and all about its relationship to Mallarmé's key poem *Un coup de dés*. It is not possible to include in a single essay the multiple interests that sustain this poetics that is like a radiant nucleus. I will look at several points of his work that enrich the discussion put forward in this study as a whole. I will start with a reiteration of the essential quality of the concrete poem. 'Piths and gists' is what the concrete poets demand of this object which

loads the noun and the verb with its meaning and which discards the adjective as merely an auxiliary element, rendering literal Huidobro's preface in *Altazor*: 'when an adjective does not give life it kills'. I want to emphasize, too, the profound reach of resistance that the concrete poem acquires through being located in historical circumstances in which Western poetry was reneging on the immediate legacy of the avant-garde and was rehearsing, on various fronts, a relapse into a poetics 'of feeling', by which I mean those aspects of lyric poetry that exist at the margins of any explicit manifestation of language as conscious of itself. The concrete poem acts as a device of duration and memory, attracting to the present traces that were constitutive of the most radical poetics of the avant-garde: linguistic experimentation, the conscious control of verbal material, and a perception of the materiality of the text as not so much—that is, not solely— about semantics. Behind the conception of the concrete poem is a consciousness of the reality of the poem that is situated firmly halfway through the twentieth century, and which has several aspects. It is a consciousness that not only highlights its own dimension of an artistic present in crisis, but also how the same approach has been dragging along since the nineteenth century— the poem's action in the middle of the euphoria of the industrial revolution, its problematic relationship with bourgeois ideology and with the ideals of social transformation—as well as the critical explosion of the socio-historic situation during the first half of the twentieth century (First and Second World Wars), and its correlation with artistic-aesthetic movements. Reference to a historical context of the mid-century in which the poem recedes into a poetics 'of feeling' is fundamental to explaining the appearance of the concrete poem as a true critical emergency. The concrete poem comes to the aid of a legacy that has rather been forgotten. The substantial transformation offered by the avant-garde with regard to the very concept of the artistic process can be seen to be conserved intact— even extrapolating from the ideal of historical change, with which it maintains a stretched relationship—twenty or thirty years on. This attitude basically consists in considering the art object as having a problematic relationship with itself and with its reception. Halfway through the twentieth century the reception of a poem cannot be the same as at the beginning. In Europe there is talk of a 'failure' of the avant-garde as a movement bound up with strategies of social change or as a dynamic that still reflects 'legitimate and totalizing' discourses, to use the vocabulary put into circulation by Lyotard.[1]

2. In Latin America—and here it is fitting to employ the distance afforded by perspective, even when the imprint of the avant-garde had a more general effect—the context is different. The concrete poets reflect upon this difference. What was 'negativity' in Europe can transmit a contrary, or at least a distinct signal, in countries that are in an ongoing position of 'emerging'. A formal repertoire in crisis—that and the tradition it brings into play—can encounter a favorable reception in cultural contexts in which tradition is not set in stone but, on the contrary, plays its cards along the lines of flexibility and openness. An emblematic text for the concrete poets in Brazil is the *Anthropophagous Manifesto* (1928) by the Brazilian poet and essayist Oswald de Andrade, a text written and conceived around difference. Let me situate this Oswaldian text properly: it is conceived around difference, not around the culpable insufficiency that can be seen in artistic mimesis, but as a form of nostalgia for what is inaccessible. Like the hand's tendency towards the unattainable, it is a gesture that is characteristic of certain Latin American cultural positions in the face of the productive centres of information—Europe, the U.S.—condemning us to the status of perpetual minors. It is a text written in a form that is ill-timed to accord with the imperialist/neo-colonial dialect, with plenty of white space between one paragraph and the next, and with a sense of humour efficient enough to rescue us from any tragic condition. Oswald de Andrade declares truths like this one: 'Before the Portuguese discovered Brazil, Brazil had discovered happiness.'[2] But this

---

[1] Jean-Francois Lyotard, *La condición postmoderna* (Madrid: Cátedra, 1998).
[2] Oswald De Andrade, 'Manifiesto antropófago', in Jorge Schwartz, *Las vanguardias latinoamericanas: textos programáticos y críticos* (Mexico City: Fondo de Cultura Económica, 1991), p. 178.

is not an elegy to some happiness that predated discovery and conquest and which intends, via humour, to disguise the ignominy of historical reality. It is about the assumption, with reference to history and reality, of a questioning and critical position towards the dominant culture, positioned nowadays as 'other', from which one can also benefit. 'Anthropophagia' is an anthropological gesture, a metaphor for the devouring of the power of the other, a ritual that is symbolic but also real in terms of its cultural consequences. It is concerned with assimilating this power and giving it a new dimension rather than only with a vengeful confrontation whose outcome is technologically predictable. What it is about, more precisely, is the appropriation of new technologies, the re-elaboration of its own usefulness, and the valuing of the new product in the international-scale cultural market. Like T. W. Adorno but with a humorous spirit, Oswald de Andrade did not lose sight of the conversion of culture to industry. This position is actively sustained by concrete poetry and by its relationship to the international poetic field. The conception of the 'hard' poem, inflexible in the rules of its construction, or 'cold', if you like, in relation to feelings, is the reply—but also the proposition—validating a culture which alters, by a process of consciousness, the mechanisms of intercultural exchange. The concrete poem has installed itself as an irrefutable presence of performative solidity and theoretical consistency on an extremely open receptive horizon and has gone on, from Brazil, to have a wide-ranging impact on Latin American poetry and on the rest of Western poetry.

3. The 'concrete phase' of Haroldian production was a crucial point in his poetics, but it was only one point. There were others, following on immediately from the abandonment of 'orthodox' concretion, and signalled by a passage from a 'concrete' conception of the poem to a fuller one of 'concreteness of poetic language'. This ritual passage allowed him, via reading, writing, and translation, to tackle the full territory of tradition, approaching it from a dialogical perspective and not as canonical reference or reverential space, common places where texts are

considered classics according to academic reading or non-specialized reception. A distancing from the orthodox concrete phase came about quite clearly from *Lacunae* (1971-1972) onwards.[3] These are texts that no longer configure an interaction between the verbal and the visual to produce a structure-form, such as was the case in the period of concrete orthodoxy. The visual quality of the sign is present in the semiotic interaction with other language figures, as is the case in those texts that use ideograms. There is a visual liberation and a semantic openness here in Haroldo de Campos's work. This formal detachment from the plasticity of the concrete poem prepared the way for the immediate writing of *Galaxias* (1973-1976), fifty 'porous' fragments written in poetic prose, which situated their author in an investigation of generic rupture, through a concept that was beyond poem or prose.[4] Here was a concept of a 'text' whose linguistic articulation would no longer depend on anterior prescriptives and in which formal necessity would generate internally which poetic mechanisms to employ. The poetic prose of *Galaxias* would use the full territory of the page. It can be observed as resembling a 'horizontal' text, in which the lines retreat to the following space not according to 'verse' or semantic finality. The end of the page indicates that the poetic-signifying specificity is not to be found there but in the intertwining that the words enter into, in their phonic relationships—plays-on-words—and in the equivalences that some signifying segments establish with others. It is about the generation of interactive semantic areas in the midst of an apparent verbal continuum, interrupted now and again by the paradigmatic repetition of certain word positions. The 'narrative style' of *Galaxias* is illusory if narration is understood to be the construction of a story, its unfolding and revelation. In the same way that the notion of verse is artificial—as proved once and for all by Mallarmé—so too is the notion of narrative. Both genres—poetry and prose—depend on a willingness to construct, on the willingness of memory, which

---

[3] Haroldo de Campos, *Xadrez de estrelas, percurso textual 1949-1974* (São Paulo: Perspectiva, 1976).
[4] Haroldo de Campos, *Galaxias* (São Paulo: Ex Libris, 1984).

is an inescapable necessity for language. *Galaxias* reveals once more that poetry is a nuclear manifestation of language acting in a nuclear way, generating spaces of condensation. Narrative illusion is broken down by the surge of these significant and privileged locations of condensation as much on the material level of language as on the semantic level. This approximation of the mechanism of Haroldo de Campos's text does not negate other aspects of it that can be easily accommodated in the ample territory of literature. In addition to being a poetic clockwork—included in this comparison are the possibilities of error in the mechanism itself i.e. the 'stoppage of time', a possibility that the text absorbs—*Galaxias* is a 'book of essays'. It makes use of generic freedom, naming itself a certain type of writing—a book of essays—but its obsessive centre is this one thing: the reflection on concreteness—that is the poetry—of language, on its material articulation, and also on what it is that poetry means semantically, as a literary ritual, and its own 'becoming' as writing. This reflection includes the role of poetry in history, its relationship with myth and its relationship with itself. It is like an arc that extends across the full horizon, from the foundations of mythology to the most minuscule point of phonetic self-reflection. Above the text, although detached from its articulation and perception, there is a metaphor: the galactic figure who substitutes for the figure of writing that situates it (writing)—in a clear homage to Mallarmé—in the physics of the sky. Neither is the biographical participation of the author excluded from this textual adventure—not everything in *Galaxias* is metaphor. It acts incessantly and corrects the official version of the text-object that states that the 'I' of the author should disappear in modern poetic writing. A lyrical dimension is also possible, says *Galaxias*: the 'I' inserts itself in an environment that correlates to real places through which the poet passes. *Galaxias* is a 'book of journeys'. The reference to Joyce, who is dialogically present in *Galaxias*, is not limited to the use of multi-levelled words, nor to the montage-creation of neologisms: in the mytho-poetics of Haroldo de Campos the poet is an Odysseus travelling through language towards a goal that is forever, infinitely deferred, guided by his own hubris, that is a vision of knowledge, which gives no respite and which constitutes—this journey, this excess—our great civilisationary metaphor.

4. The adventure of poetic knowledge that Haroldo de Campos's poetry represents can not, by dint of its multiplicity, be confined to historical epochal poetics, nor divided into historical philosophical segments. His poetics is a trans-poetics that crosses classical and modern poetry, baroque and avant-garde, the Enlightenment and the present in which we live. It is a poetics of 'nowness'—a term taken directly by the poet from Walter Benjamin—that corresponds to the present moment, not post-modern but rather post-utopian, to use the poet's words. Guided by Oswald de Andrade's anthropophagous sign, it absorbs and incorporates different poetic moments, recreating them in order to decipher them. For Haroldo de Campos all true poetry is metalinguistic to a greater or lesser degree, complying with that function of language as perceived by Roman Jakobson which hinges on the 'palpable aspect' of signs. That is to say, all real poetry gives evidence of its materiality: it is, by definition, self-reflective. Only modern poetry represents the ecstatic moment of this revelation. What Haroldo de Campos wants from Dante, in 'transcreating' it—a word that designates a special concept of translation, that is a translation of the form that seeks to rescind the 'iconic' in language, present in the poetry of whichever epoch—what he wants from Goethe, from Homer, and what he was looking for in the Ecclesiastes (to enumerate just a few emblematic names from his vast translation oeuvre)—are signs of the 'concreteness' that poetic language displays. In Latin America, besides Huidobro, Vallejo and Girondo, he was particularly inspired by Octavio Paz's *Blanco* (1966), a poem that he translated into Portuguese in a process he named *Transblanco* (1986).[5] *Blanco* interested Haroldo de Campos because of its superlative characteristics as a metalinguistic poem. The unearthing in this text of the possibilities of an *ex nihilo*

---

[5] Haroldo De Campos and Octavio Paz, *Transblanco* (São Paulo: Siciliano, 1984).

creation, a creation 'out of nothingness', the evocation of the Mallarméan adventure in Latin American poetry of the second half of the twentieth century, could not fail to take hold of Haroldo de Campos' generous fascination. For his part, Octavio Paz had recognized the influence of concrete poetry on his more experimental poetry, on *Blanco* and on *Topoemas* (1967). In the name of the resulting Portuguese poem—no longer *Blanco* but *Transblanco*—Haroldo de Campos clearly enunciates his poetics of translation. Translation, for him, is not a second-hand poetics. On the contrary, following Novalis, he considers the translator to be the poet of poets, one who needs to re-tread the original creative path in order to be able to create its equivalent in another language. Transcreation does not rehash the original poem: literally, it makes another poem, through seeking a formal equivalent of the text that serves as a base, while still maintaining its spirit. Inherent in the idea of 'transcreation' is a conception of the poetic work in relation to tradition that Haroldo de Campos inherits from Ezra Pound. It deals with the Poundian motto *Make It New*. (The meaning is not 'Make It Again'—Why 'again'?—but precisely, in fact, *Make It New*.) The idea is none other than to take the present as a point of departure, from which to revise the past. This is a very different position to the obedience that the traditional school of thought teaches, with its 'journeys' to the time of the work, as if in this 'topos' of literary memory something exists—a date, a register, a sign, a level—that does not depend on a punctual active reading in the present. However, this notion of 'the new', not euphemistic but rather real, is a long way away in Haroldo de Campos from becoming a cult to the present. The present is nothing more nor less than the unique real time of writing and consequently that of reading. Another aspect is the poet's aspiration, his demand for a time in which the truth about the human condition—evanescent, always sought-after—is accomplished: the yearning for justice. Meanwhile, in the ethos of 'nowness', the re-vision of the past from the optic of the present is asserted. Recognition of the jubilant or agonizing dimensions of our time—'in the present', agony in relation to a utopian perspective—prevails as a way of not betraying what was given to us, that is this present that makes it possible to see things in a certain way, to articulate them precisely.[6] *Finismundo: a última viagem* (1990), a poem by Haroldo de Campos which again takes up the last stage of Odysseus's hubris, makes use of a line from Dante, in which the navigator of knowledge is condemned, as an epigram—'per voler veder traspassó il segno' [in his quest to know he missed the sign]—and situates, in precise hendecasyllabic Danteesque terms, what is in reality Haroldo de Campos's poetic adventure, always close to the hubris of his admired 'hybrids'. But since he wants to (re)view the poetry in the present state, there is no hubris. This classic Odysseus and this post-utopian Faust, which Haroldo de Campos makes his own, through his personal mytho-poetics, are his 'personae'; they are masks, symbolic presences. There is no excess in his evocation. He does not argue with prohibitive designations nor with now retired gods. What he delivers to his readers, secularly, is poetry. There is no sin here (there is no Dante who judges). He wants to make the reader conscious of 'the dignity of poetry', to use the words of Lezama Lima, another valid interlocutor of Haroldo de Campos. Or is this a condition of Latin American genius, of the 'American expression', of this 'horror of emptiness' which lives like a goblin ('*duende*') in the green foliage—the pretension of knowing, of tasting, everything? If the luxury of the image frees Lezama Lima from any hubris, the minuscule phonetic devotion of Haroldo de Campos and his capacity to elevate it to a spiritual dimension as another precise form of celebrating creation should—it occurs to me—be fit to serenade the best of the gods.

5. And, if any doubt should remain about the poet being compromised, here is the fact of an action—a historical, current, present day action—part of an actual socio-political juncture that had a real existence: Haroldo de Campos wrote the slogan for a publicity campaign for Luiz Inácio Lula de Silva, a candidate for the P.T. (Workers' Party), shortly before the presidential elections

---

[6] Haroldo de Campos, *Finismundo: A última viagem* (Ouro Preto: Tipografia de Fundo de Ouro Preto, 1990).

in Brazil, which he finally won. Is taking part not, perhaps, one of the poet's functions in this extraordinarily demanding newness in which we live? This is the same poet who sought concreteness in the expression of Dante, in that of Homer and in that of Goethe. Poetry makes solidarity 'concrete'.

Translated by Ruth Hemus

The Present of Martínez Rivas

1. To speak of a poetic present—or of a poetic 'now'—means referring to the horizon of utopian collapse that unfolded throughout the twentieth century and that, even though it finds its final realization with the 'fall of real socialism' (or of the wall of real socialism in Berlin), does not find its reflective text—philosophical, aesthetic, social—until the publication in 1979 of Lyotard's *The Post-modern Condition*. The philosophical and aesthetic reflections are integrated into artistic practice with an almost modern naturalness. The point now is to register the results of that collapse, not its causes. The search for the causes implies a retrospective look that would lead us to the beginnings of industrial modernity and their impact on art and poetry. Instead, the 'now' delimits a space of proximity, that takes place close by, and which empowers or encloses us. We can identify the stylistic features of this poetic 'now': irony, sarcasm, bitterness, disenchantment, consciousness of impossibilities, mistrust in art and its liberating attributes. On rare occasions—although it does happen: 'El desierto de Atacama' [The Atacama Desert] (1979), *Hospital Británico* [British Hospital] (1986)—we find displays of hope, wagers for a way out of the conditioning order of things. Poetry is written in the present with reality as a starting point. The distancing from reality is a tactical device, as much as 'taking distance' from the work is a device. There are poems that are prisoners of reality, as there are poems that are prisoners of self-reflection. These can be limiting but also dialogical possibilities, reference points for the poem to unfold in its objectivity. Poetic language acknowledges those points of reference as evidence: there is a history that cannot be avoided, a history of the poem that presents itself punctually in writing. In a second instance, there is a plurality of poetic forms that interact simultaneously, proving at this moment that artistic form is not in question. The use of multiple poetic forms—just like the in the general

milieu of art there is an indiscriminate use of forms—reveals that the 'culture industry' does not demand new forms. If by new forms we understand those resulting from art's experimentation with itself. There is a *Babelification* of forms. After art's successive 'deaths'—announced first by Hegel in the nineteenth century and repeated by the avant-garde movements of the twentieth— the rebirth of art shows in practice the following possible images: that of a formal hybrid; that of a crossbreeding of contents— keeping in mind in this view the tradition of prestige and bloodlines—and also the image of a body that registers on itself the unequivocal signs of the passage from death to rebirth, and which offers those as evidence.[1] In the worst case, this is an image of a moment of cultural confusion that art itself makes manifest. If linguistic experimentation constituted a dominant line in most twentieth century art, in Latin American poetry there were individual works that in their moment, perceived retrospectively from this impasse, acted as early symptoms of what would later be a generalized artistic malaise.

2. *La insurrección solitaria* [*The Solitary Insurrection*] (1953) by Carlos Martínez Rivas (1924–1998) fulfilled the function of situating the space of poetic discussion outside any logical, formal, or thematic precepts. The title is an emblem of the contradiction in which the poet acts. 'Insurrection' is a word that remits to sense of plurality, 'solitary' is an individual possibility or condition. The emblematic title could also refer to a place: the place of the poet, the place of 'the solitary insurrection'. There are two poles of attraction: the multitude and the subject. The poem is a pendulum that comes and goes from one to the other. And it even is a state of the poet in the world, a stance: an outcry reduced to itself. It is igniting a fire, as a general proposal, and its immediate quelling. To repeat, it is not about a situation but of a conditioning stance. More than to a juncture it seems to remit to ontology, to the poet's category of being. If this remitted to a juncture, it would be the long problematic juncture of the

---

[1] Dino Fromaggio, *La 'muerte del arte' y la estética* (Mexico City: Grijalbo, 1992), pp. 20-21.

poet and his place in the field of modernity, between social participation and chosen exclusion. At the moment of its publication, the title situates the book in the coordinates of an individualistic scepticism in the face of history: the 'cold' war, the restoration of the capitalist West, bipolarization. It documents a dual state of things. However, it is still the projection in time of what was the poet's disjunctive in the nineteenth century, between the agitator (Victor Hugo) and the recluse in artistic forms and the abyss of the word (Mallarmé); between the part that bourgeois consciousness demanded from the artist—its 'madman' that rebels against it but tells it its truth—and the one that cultivates an aristocratic distance, keeping in mind this apparent contradiction. The truth of the stance of *La insurrección solitaria*, is precisely the poet's contradiction in that phase of post-industrial capitalism and his capacity to manifest it. The 'textual ego' takes distance vis-à-vis the logic of the system. He is neither 'integrated' nor 'apocalyptic'. He is a critic situated at the margins of worldly noise. He criticizes social values; not society from its systematic establishment, but its values. He is a dissident; or more clearly, a disobedient. There are no new values proposed, no suggestion of an alternative. From the radicalism of the 'ego', of clear neo-Romantic lineage, the bourgeois veil is lifted, a qualifying adjective that in the middle of the twentieth century still functions as aggression. *La insurrección solitaria* allows us to see this juncture clearly pointed out by Andrew Bowie, who remarks that modern art finds itself between the desire for subjective self-expression, the fear that such self-expression is empty of any collective meaning, and the danger it constitutes for the future existence of any collective formation.[2] In the meantime, in 1953, Martínez Rivas knew about the poet's necessary separation from the consciousness of a class—the bourgeoisie—which formulated the sense of its existence—and not the reasoning behind the production of material goods—through art. Yet not from all art, but art conceived as a manifestation of the sublime which, as it is well

---

[2] Andrew Bowie, *Aesthetics and Subjectivity: from Kant to Nietzsche* (Manchester: Manchester University Press, 1990), p. 34.

known, finds its most meaningful expression in music. I am making reference here to a text that integrates a character of true poetics into *La insurrección solitaria*: 'Memoria para el año de viento inconstante' ['Memory for the Year of Inconstant Wind']. The poem opens thus:

> Sí. Ya sé.
> Ya sé yo que lo que os gustaría es una Obra maestra.
> Pero no la tendréis.
> De mí no la tendréis.
> Aunque se vuelva, comentando, algún maestro
> del humor entre vosotros. —Poco trabajo le
> costará cumplir...—
> Aunque sepa hasta qué extremo las amáis.
> Se cómo amáis la Música.
> No la de los negros, por supuesto. Ni la guitarra
> a lo rasgado, por tientos, esa
> brisa seca de uñas y plata. Ni el endiablado
> son de la Múcura que está en el suelo, o Rosa de
> Castilla
> con su largo alarido al comienzo...
> sino BACH!
> Últimamente sobre todo Juan-Sebastián Bach.[3]
>
> [Yes. I know.
> I know that what you would like is a Masterpiece.
> But you shan't have it.
> You shall not have it from me.
> Even if some master of mood, over his shoulder,
> commented among you: it would cost him little to comply...
> Even though I know to what extremes you love them.
> I know how you adore Music.
> Not Black, of course. Nor the ripping
> Guitar, *por tientos*, that

---

[3] 'Memoria para el año de viento inconstante', in Milán, Eduardo and Lumbreras, Ernesto, eds., *Prísitna y última piedra: antología de poesía hispanoamericana presente* (Mexico City: Aldus, 1999), p. 3

Dry breeze of fingernails and silver, nor the devilish
Sound of Múcura on the ground, or the Rose of
Castile
With its long howl at the beginning...
But BACH!
Lately above all Johann Sebastian Bach.]

The necessary principle of the denial of art in the face of an ignominious present, formulated theoretically by Adorno among others, acquires a practical translation in the poem's content level. There is no 'darkening of the formal signs' that would lead to the darkening of the thematic proposal. A poetically orthodox denial would indicate a transmission not thematically but formally obscured. Martínez Rivas draws on the thematic clarification as a device to signal one of art's major problems according to the aesthetic judgment of a class—not the artist's judgment—that is the 'finished work': a synthesis of the human spirit manifested in its splendor and an offering to a receiver that takes it as an equal. What gets broken in the poem is the dialogue among pairs, the exchange, the reciprocity. The return of the gift—this gift the bourgeoisie redeems as the value of genius as it pretends to own it by becoming its sole receiver—does not take place. The aesthetic-communicative circuit is broken. The poet does not fulfil his function. Not to satisfy the aesthetic demand of a class negates the class itself, particularly if that class legitimates its own existence through art, as is the case of the modern bourgeoisie. The denial functions as the disqualification of the ultimate purpose of that class. The bourgeoisie does not have the legitimacy to demand a distillation of art that is the masterpiece. The secularization of art is literal in Martínez Rivas. It is not the possibility of reception in a dialogue whose mythical interlocutors pointed to the gods as receivers of the message. It is the absence of interlocution. The interlocutor's lost prestige is exposed here as a conscience that seeks to appropriate the modes in which art circulates. Martínez Rivas goes further, he moves from the denial of the demand of a class to the denial of what that class demands. The 'master work' comes into play here not as a given value but as a value in itself. Here the reflection is in fact mythical. The 'divine fire' does not translate into song. And if it does, its achievement is imperfect, half way. Bach is an emblem of perfection, of what is valuable in art. It stands for aesthetic accomplishment and the realization of the gift. On the other hand, Black music, the guitar '*a lo rasgado*'—that of the gypsies—this adds to their musical 'elementariness' the 'singularity' of race. It is music of the intellect in its baroque distillation—its construction—against the music of expression, of direct transmission, immediately directed to the body. 'Major' music against 'minor' music, 'classic' against 'popular', 'definitive' art against 'provisional' art, 'spirit' against 'flesh', dominant ideology against ideological marginality. Or, simply—as if there could be any simplicity in this matter—of art against life, with Martínez Rivas clearly taking the side of the latter. We are no longer dealing with the preaching unification of art and life, driving engine of the avant-garde movements, the criticism of art from the side of life at the beginning of the twentieth century, but rather a de-sublimating practice of the artistic function and the poetry's landing on the convulsive terrain of history. It is a proposal for and from the concreteness of what exists in the non-transcendental condition of mortality. It is a taking of sides for the immediate, for what palpitates *here*. A principle of similitude is exercised—not of homogeneity—before the same provisional destiny, in defence of fragility and of what has been left behind: life as what is born and dies with no more aspiration than a transitory stay. Without a doubt this is about a response, in poetic terms, to the nineteenth century's philosophical dominant discourse—of the 'great narratives' as confirmed by Lyotard—and its translation into a socio-cultural praxis, although not with the ambition for social transformation as it was manifested by art at the beginnings of the twentieth century.[4] Rather it is a will to rescue what is individual and singular, what is one's own gathered through experience. This response can only mistrust the immersions of intellectual reasoning in the artistic milieu and the regulating self-legitimizing function that such immersion

---

[4] Jean-Francois Lyotard, *La condición postmoderna* (Barcelona: Gedisa, 1980).

entails. Martínez Rivas opposes to the world of the masterpiece that of raw Nature, half-tamed, on its way to take a form, a world constantly emerging on the outskirts of reason and verification, a world of unknown functions that explain themselves, a continuous metamorphosis. The second part of 'Memoria para el año de viento inconstante', that of 'life', confronts the first, that of 'the masterpiece', according to the description of what is alive acting as an uncontrollable mechanism:

> terco mundillo del amanecer.
> La pululante línea de la imperfección y el anonimato.
>
> Más informe en el año del hombre y dudosa que
> en el año exterior
> los renacuajos moviéndose sin dignidad,
> que la crisálida de una abeja en su célula
> cuando no es sino un poco de saliva ciega y moho,
> que esas medusas que olvidó el mar
> aún sin hacer, translúcidas de asco.

> [Stubborn little world of dawn.
> Pullulating line of imperfection and anonymity.
>
> More shapeless in the year of man and doubtful
> Than in the exterior year
> The tadpoles moving without dignity,
>
> Than the chrysalis of a bee in its cell
> When it is nothing more than blind spit and mould,
> Than those jellyfish forgotten by the sea
> Still without doing, revoltingly transparent.]

In reality, the opposition is between the consolidated and the not yet consolidated, between a 'work'—oeuvre—that presupposes an achieved formalization, and what still exists without one. What exists as the latter cannot be negotiated, appropriated, or exchanged. It is not latency, the total availability of what is *in potentia* without actually being born, but rather a beginning, the recent beginning, an immediate birth captured in the tension of its present moment. This is the stance: the constant beginning, the utopia of the recently born in high contrast with the 'finished' work, in both senses of this word. The poet cannot avoid the becoming but can capture the instant, re-send what has been formalized to its condition as a project only. He thus turns form into a permanent project. The mobility of nature in its mechanism is the image proposed for the form of the poem. In Martínez Rivas there is no predetermined poetic form. It is configured by the poem's necessity. The *colloquializing* use of language—not colloquial anymore, like in Parra, where language delivers itself to the reader by the similitude of speeches and codes—appeals frequently to the ellipsis as a device of discontinuity, and it constantly refers to the cultural universe as a given known fact. This 'familiarity' with the cultural referents obscures the transmission of what is communicated, it denies complicity, and rescues what is properly poetic at the point of being transformed into pure denotation.

Martínez Rivas tricks the reader, he gives knowledge that the reader does not have and puts him in evidence. This reveals the reader's desiring character as nothing more than that: desire for the 'masterpiece', without knowing what to do with it, desire's incompetence, the need to redeem itself in what it doesn't know. The clarification of meaning is interrupted by an intermittent apparition of an objectivity without concessions, that emerges and blocks reflection. The dialogue that appeared possible at the beginning of the poem was not really feasible. The reader and poet are not peers. Martínez Rivas retakes Baudelaire's motif of the reader's hypocrisy and situates it in the category of a consciousness of a class. In challenging the stature of the 'master work'—'eagerness for a personal holocaust', he calls it— he puts in check the dimension of the aesthetic sublime. This is the insurrection. What remains is what is specifically poetic, its characteristic solitude.

Translated by Antonio Ochoa

2

An Essay on Poetry

Chapter One
The Intimate Power

If poetry is discontinuity, if it is intermittent perception, the language of the essay is also discontinuous, the perception that it captures intermittent. This condition of freedom in the essay resembles that of language in poetry, the freedom of language when it draws near to what the poet understands as poetry. The freedom of the essay is a topic in itself. There is a way of conceptualizing the poem as that moment in which writing allows us to know what it is doing—why, when it comes to a crossroads, it chooses one road and not the other. There is a crossroads in every poem. In a great poem there are multiple crossroads. The metaphor is always that of going, of getting going. I don't want to get into the motif of the journey because getting into that is truly getting in: one does not exit the adventure of knowledge through just any door. Ulysses, for example. The greatest pleasure in every poem is to perceive the choice of one road and not the other, the wager on the sole direction that will guide us on a path we only intuit and don't necessarily know. In any case, this is modern: tracing palm-by-palm as if measuring with one's hands something that does not withstand the weight of hands nor their rubbing. If it were a serious undertaking, we might call it 'measuring the abyss palm by palm.' But it isn't serious. After finishing or abandoning the route down the chosen road, a poem can take up the abandoned road again. There we find out that it wasn't abandoned. There we find out that it was only a momentary delay. It was on hold. We don't begin again because we are aware of the other road's presence: it smells like poplars alongside a stone wall. We simply pick up the trail of a possibility that kept its time intact while we went with another time in a different place. This is the modern:

all the roads. As the nineteenth century advanced we learned to write in short sentences. As we approached the end of the century the short sentence began to reign in a realm that had opened up; *A Season in Hell, A Throw of the Dice*. In this last poem there remains the punctual, painful awareness of a fall not to the centre but without a centre: the song falls to the bottom of the mockingbird. Mallarmé the mockingbird invented the poem-dilemma. Dilemma, not riddle. There is nothing to figure out, there is no trail to pick up for those who are searching, the bloodhound critic is led off track by his sense of smell—the sense of smell was an old reality, an ancient ritual that stopped working. And the bloodhound critic cannot help but construct an immense, empty theatre out of that poem, the oldest poem in idealist lyric poetry. If the poem-dilemma has been posited—we are in 1897—the rules for the poem-dilemma must be invented. The poem-dilemma is a constant choice—one always chooses, doesn't always win, doesn't always lose, it's a trade-off, the rescue doesn't always work: look at the Mississippi. Look now at the water over New Orleans. The criminal stupidity, muddy water drowning the cradle of jazz with jazz's baby inside, displaced water over jazz's black man, black woman, and little black boy, the tarantula of water over the birth. What remains does not imply complete stability, a circle retraced around the fire, the night of the first words where we were speakers and listeners, words supported from underneath by the heat of coals. An honest system of reference cannot *not* allude to that poem. I don't want to try not to. That Mallarmé invented the poem-dilemma means: Mallarmé invented the precise register—this is the *lento*, we are proceeding by parts, step by step—of the poem-dilemma. An operatic, elliptic bird does pirouettes with the ellipsis: it does not add or take away anything. This also is modern: to record everything, not throw anything out, before recycling we would record every step as if inventing a memory of what has been discarded. Is there another way? *The age demanded a*—discontinuous—*image*. Walter Benjamin's *Arcades Project* is the testimony of someone who saw well: that implacable wave of industrial capitalism leaves a few fermenting spots by the wayside like men who died before the First World War and who will appear during the First World War, the site of catastrophe where the spirit of Europe castrates itself. We have to stop there, survey them. We have to contemplate that. It's a subterranean connection, a dark passage traversed by many people. It's a nuclear anthill, by which I mean an atom ignited yet intermittent. And *stop* is the word. The subterranean word of capitalism—this is seen very well in the rise of industry—the word that waits everywhere but that is not *vertigo, velocity, contradiction, mass*, that cumulative series of superficial sparks that slide together on the complicit thread of a neon lamp and that seem to define everything in the end, is *stop*. It's in the texts, it's in the texts of the sages, it's in the silence of the sages that Jorge Reichmann often cites: *stop*. It's an always-underlying word, it has always been there and it still doesn't reach us. The sages' lips are too small for silence not to escape, small lips that cannot be fleshy like those of lusted-after women who don't know what silence is. In this sense the *arcade* is a stopping, something parallel to the hasn't-been that calls out, the thing that was left flapping its wings in the background but that nothing—the cry from a beak, chicks, nest, straw—can lead us to call a bird. The arcade, the many people, the multitude, the amassed lot, the anthill of the arcade is a messianic desire—or a certainty: [Gustavo Adolfo Bécquer's] 'volverán las oscuras golondrinas' [the dark sparrows will return] in Cirlot's Bachian variations. A poem is an arcade. An arcade where the crossroads always appears. In a great poem there are several crossroads. 'I've made a poem about nothing' (*Farey un vers de dreyt nien*), a poem that is admirable by definition, begins in open allusion to the crossroads: 'It came to me while I was sleeping / on my horse' [English translation by Leonard Cottrell]. I translated this poem for the journal *Vuelta* in the early nineties. In my experience it is linked to my beginnings in the Humanities Faculty in Montevideo, to my Provençal classes with Guido Zannier. My version was reproduced in the journal *El poeta y su trabajo* [The Poet and His Work], no. 1, Fall 2000, Mexico City. That passage from Guillaume de Poitiers is a mental landscape into which one can docilely fall, and in that state become suspended, which is the ideal moment for writing poetry. Not so much the instant: the suspension. Even in the current trend of radical poetics in Argentina—poetics of the colloquial that have learned the lesson of Nicanor Parra, the only Latin American poet who really changed the conception and attitude of poetry in what we have lived of the twentieth century—one reads by suspension. Even in the street, in the mimesis of spoken language that is called street, congestion, traffic, noise, there is a parcelling-up, a will—an obligatory will—for restriction that the reader accesses. In this metonymic space created by force, arbitrarily great or small according to the author's capacities for cold or heat, the seasons of the year, the economy of the house, the price of crude on the international market—the crude which so much, in its name, recalls the truth—a metaphorical construction rises up, growing paler as the poem advances—seasoned, made alert by the threat—in its fading towards decomposition. That ritual remains: the ritual of the decomposition of the poem, decay without being handled like that of an untouched peach, the losing of oneself in some passage that is always losing oneself in oneself, disappearing into one's depths—that's something: rebirth is only a metaphor that suggests a different appearance—in order to be reborn. The other style that is already out there is babelization. It's just that there are no real referents there: 'no one talks that way.' No one wants to remember the detonation where the languages are dispersed. The referents are textual, idiomatic. Pieces that don't imply a dismembered ontology, a dream of reconfiguration, or the initial utopia of a beginning. It isn't translation into the language of a shattered consciousness. It's the simple and straightforward construction of forms without mourning the loss of some ideal form. A cold act. With heat, the mourning isn't yet cold. One accepts the game. The act depends on the intensity of each person's reading, the extent to which it mends languages. Polyglots, gluttons of language around the long, mosaic-walled dining halls of poorhouses. The indigence of the word is not the same thing as the word of the indigent. Consciousness of language as indigence is generally a topic for the poetry of the first world, Europe or the United States, there where poverty is scarce. When indigence is widespread the babelic gluttony sounds like leftovers at the bottom of the pot: potatoes, carrots, string beans, greens, squash, and a few bones floating on the surface of the water. New Orleans, a city flooded by those who haven't given anything. It's a linguistic collage, the experience of many worlds if each language gives an image of the world, many coexisting images of worlds, only cropped to the extreme. It's a different amalgamation, a different grouping. But it cannot be taken too seriously except as the symptom of a foreseen illness. What was foreseen was the sticky residue in the sentence, the effort to stick. There was that impossibility of forgetting, our version of the ancestral tam-tam. Ancestral? Of what ancestors? Joyce is the master, a happy truism that has been stretched by what the experimentalist disciples of the twentieth century have been able to do with him: stretch him like an elastic shadow, tug at the four horses of his echo from each cardinal point. Better than nothing. Or no: there is a moment-before evoked by the concept of *antepalabra* [*before the word*] which stands for what can always be reinvented precisely because it is unverifiable. It's not a place, this point before the word doesn't exist. It isn't a source, it isn't a spring, nor a fountain: it's an unverifiable point, a point like a name, a signal that is as familiar as it is impossible to find, I insist: not a place, a non-place. Valente did well in naming that instance of a possible starting-over, with the full awareness of the risk of mythification that mysticism shields with its aura: knowing that 'babbling' isn't babbling anymore. Although it may never be what it seems—the desired word always has a different appearance, a displacement that occurs in the mass-produced, shiny mythopoetics of the present, its roof just emerging from the rain of the car-wash; steamed poetics, garbage narcissism with no connection to the original myth, a hackneyed myth that acts as the prefix to what one can't pin down because it's impossible even if 'poetics' were its 'natural' release, its intimate, crazy, and crazier 'destiny': this unsettling provisional quality of all of life in our present must be recognized, but the logic of the poetic sense was always to return to the steadfast word, the dolmen, the totem, the monolith among the monkeys, the immovable landmark that loosens its ties, opens its sails, casts off its moorings, takes its people to the streets, and is the understandable dissolution, the thousand meanings that threw everything off: it was to bring back the logical movement—although what it seems to be might not exist, although the desired purification of time in time might not happen, the impulse to go and search, to look back, is still there. It is clear, obdurately clear, as the perfect invisible column pardons not seeing what must be seen and seeing what must not be seen, that there is nothing to be said. Poetry was an approach to what we wanted to say. Now it's an approach to the way in which we say. In this way, saying can only revolve around itself, no matter how much the space of verbal movement tends to widen, to turn itself into an environment rather than a context: in this way speech can only be a spinning top. And our dreams, an infinitely revolving top. Elsewhere I have called the poetics that jumped over this implacable reality, a reality like an eternal valley that one cannot avoid, 'poetics of return,' poetics that pretended to come back as something other than the desire for a source: as a movement of contemporary ignorance capable of petrifying any consciousness that falls into its mechanism of repetition. It became difficult, then, to talk about historical art, about historical form, about the historical word: an entire century—the twentieth—wanted to leave history. There were a couple of doors available for the escape: the quotidian one, the here-and-now, only slow, eating ice cream, counting on the risk of the banalization of existence, of concentrated frivolity, of the control of the spirit that is called consensus, under the permanent rain or threat of irreversible cretinism: touching the ground as an epiphany or a breath of the promised ether, the air of the gods made for no one's nose, jell-o instead of ambrosia: in any case, 'nothing more will ever happen.' Everything thoroughly washed down with an elemental, mind-numbing ideological cocktail. Along the side of the paragraph, but with an insistent ability to filter in, hunger, poverty, hopelessness, ignorance, decay, every kind of irreparable degradation. To write is no longer to be protected from the margin, to be inside as a sign of belonging, a lineage woven of fine thread: 'I talk with Petrarch. And you?' Rigorous modernity wrote unaccompanied, *a cappella*. We write with an over-flowing margin. The door of everyday life. Because there is also colloquial poetry, which corresponds to the satisfied cherishing of the everyday, the one that won the poetic battle of the century, the underlying battle waged between 'pure' language and language 'of the street': language 'of the street' won. North American poetry played a fundamental role in the possibility of using that language in twentieth-century Latin American poetry. Even when that language belongs to a much wider, epochal sphere of usage, that of modernity, it descends to Latin American poetry from Europe, where it went to thank Laforgue. (Jules Laforgue, 1860-1887, born in Montevideo and deceased in France, has a monument in the section of Montevideo known as *Ciudad Vieja*, next to Isidore Ducasse, the Count of Lautréamont, and Jules Supervielle, represented by a little bronze boat, a frigate really, with these words engraved underneath: 'For the poets that Uruguay gave to France.' Poetry is like love: one gives what one doesn't have, so says French thought according to the Valéry-Lacan tradition. But it is true: to Supervielle we owe the balance of irony, to Lautréamont the power to startle, and to Laforgue a revolution in poetic language. Not bad.) It could have been localized by turning its gaze, as the Nicaraguan poets did, to the border with the United States, which was right there. But Ezra Pound, like Eliot, had gone to Europe with 80 dollars (Pound with 80 dollars, not Eliot), and like Eliot he says in one of his cantos (in one of Pound's cantos, not Eliot's: in Canto CXVI, to be precise): 'And I have learned more from Jules / (Jules Laforgue) since then / depths in him.' José Coronel Urtecho, Carlos Martínez Rivas, and Ernesto Cardenal, to name a few, know what I'm talking about. What is true is that in the twentieth century the colloquial laurels went to Nicanor Parra, not for privileging the use of colloquial language, but rather because he like no one else, like no one else in Latin America, problematized the poem, poetry, and the poet. Colloquial language and the language of the street are often confused. Though some (whole social groups, usually marginalized) might speak the same way in the house as on the street, there is no conflict of interest in these modes. The conflict comes with the 'other' language, poetic *par excellence*—or rather, *par tradition*—language orchestrated according to a poetic conception of auratic language (there are, always, exceptions, apparitions, intermittences, dragonflies: satiric poetry, the Medieval romance, which is considered the 'lyrical dawn' in the West, the *jarchas*, the Galician-Portuguese *cantigas de amigo*, and, once we're in the house, the Provençal poetry of Guillaume de Poitiers, François Villon—in this last case, the word 'house' is only an organized metaphor for shared existence, not for a home nor for shelter, nothing *inhabitable*: if the poet is *on the outside*, as Maurice Blanchot affirms, Villon is doubly so: once for being a poet, and again for being persecuted). In modernity poetic language went from being a language considered worn out from use, insofar as the Enlightenment makes it neoclassical, a certain Romanticism—undoubtedly the German variety—solemnifies it, Symbolism undermines it and reproaches its ineffectiveness, to being an abandoned language, as if belonging to a past age. Its memory is preserved in the texts considered canonical. And, in the light of the exorbitant use of linguistic colloquialism, it has become an increasingly dangerous absence as it makes itself seen in an astonishing way in certain texts of present-day poetry, especially those that are on the edge of non-poetry or those that incorporate that dysfunction as a point from which to critique the creative process itself. The aforementioned difficulty of calling for historicity in poetic art, especially in terms of contemporary form, does not come, obviously, from colloquial poetry or from street language. In colloquial poetry it is language that organizes poetic form, or, in other words, the form is organized depending on the kind of language used. Straddling the formal search organized from language and the call for interaction with the best inherited poetic tradition, it is concrete poetry that invites historicity to the poetic adventure. The second door of entry after the twentieth century's flight from history, a door situated parallel to the quotidian door, is the atemporal door, the eternal door in that it is always open, eternal in that it is always 'there,' always available like a sonnet or any fixed form. Always, always, always: it is the consolation of art and quite possibly of any alternative to transcendence. Concrete poetry tries to obstruct the flight from history. Concrete language does not fight with colloquial language, which can achieve a high level of concreteness. We already have the examples. In reality, the process of poetic language's decay depends a great deal, for its verification, on the angle from which one views lived existence. To live according to the principle of banality or under the sign of consensual virtuality, a rootless, fleeting existence of an individual condemned to immanence and therefore to him or herself, every transformative horizon declared impossible—as seen by the dominant discourse, obviously—in exchange for an endless stream of commodities—satisfiers that are unlikely to satisfy—professionalization and a recycled reiteration of the imminent threat—until it stops being imminent and actually becomes a reality—viruses, terrorism, and pandemics are the promises of the current world order that protects the world situated under this order, not including the margins. From this view of existence, there is a demand for the purposeless purpose of poetry to produce something of substance. This demand, legitimate for its point of origin—the inconsistency of life and the inconsolable awareness of that inconsistency—rarely directs its call, or, in the best-case scenario, its critique, to the right recipient. Once again, an artistic practice takes responsibility for life's failure. Neither poetry and its varieties of language nor the different ways of approaching the poetic phenomenon are inconsistent: it is lived life that does not satisfy. Or it satisfies by way of too-superficial goods that, in highly degraded societies, don't allow for the basic assumption of the human condition. Poetry as an experience of language, as a constant advance toward linguistic limits, an artistic participant in an existence stunted in its capacity for transformation, changes its sign and transforms itself into its opposite: what was art-in-process becomes art of accompaniment, what used to be provocation of perception, sensibility, and intelligence—in sum: the widening of consciousness—becomes an unsure, unfulfilling practice. Art stopped being otherness and became sameness, stationed on the edge of existence. Play becomes synonymous with frivolity, a patent forgetting of its original condition as ritual. Serious poetry is needed for existence, whether frivolous, or threatening, or lacking in prospects for change. In any case, we attempt to return to the 'only meta-physical activity after the death of God,' the charge given to art by Nietzsche in full awareness of the seriousness of its implications. In the presence of such a *clamor*—'clamor' as a paraphrase of Jorge Guillén, as the enchanted manifestation of a spiritual act of enchantment that no longer enchants or at least not as we wish it would, so long as one keeps in mind the camp of interested reception in art when it cannot be a mediatory phenomenon; according to logic poetry itself is an effectively non-existent 'worldly clamor' [*clamor mundial*]: everyone's attention is elsewhere—seriousness and safety, the stability of forms are the camouflage of a *need for meaning* that one misses in poetry and modern art, whose consideration implicitly brings with it a good dose of risk. In literature, the novel should have its own consideration: its language, from the time of its bourgeois formulation, is a language of accompaniment. This isn't the Ortegan question of the 'dehumanization of art'—or it still is, in some way, after all: it is literal un-satisfaction, the denunciation of art's insufficiency, the location of a space 'that it doesn't reach,' in the sense that it does not fulfil. We must distinguish this from the insufficiency of meaning that is sought out, taken to its limit: 'Dada doesn't mean anything' (Tzara), which is a specifically historical manifestation and an insufficiency of meaning in that there is no meaning, that it is missing. But meaning, with regard to its absence in art, is not the problem. If we unpack the term, nineteenth-century poetry—Symbolism and Romanticism—and part of the poetry of the first three decades of the twentieth century, *lacked meaning*, as the above-quoted words of Tzara attest. *The Waste Land* embodies a *lack of meaning* even as it tries to demonstrate this absence: it fights against absence with absence, not plenitude. Unable to escape a last-ditch mimesis—the same thing happens with *A Throw of the Dice*—poetry reproduces what it wants to criticize, at least that poetry whose subject matter precedes the internal organization of its language. What is strange is that in contemporary post-modern times, accustomed as we are to various degrees of privation, we still demand completeness from art. The explanation of what we now identify as *lack of meaning* is to be found in our own existence.

Chapter Two

Find the Old Dream of Play in Exile

Outside of the outside, exile is an entrance to poetry. For one who had already entered (I had) it is the ratification of the entrance. To write poetry is to be exiled before going into exile. 'Going into exile': this is an *abysmal figure*, a vertical axis of expression. Like falling without ever touching the ground: 'a falling that does not find the ground,' an expulsion into ether, birth into the dominion of immensity. Should 'immensity' be capitalized? It prefigures a door through which one enters the exit. Is there a doorman at the exit? A guard at the entrance? They haven't been seen. Perhaps because exile is separation, not only from the country of origin; a permanent separation, exile separates itself from exile at an unchanging 'vanishing point.' Perhaps because of this it is made up of nostalgia, a nostalgia for community, a nostalgia for surroundings that misses a ring of poplars, a pair of hands warming themselves by the fire. If it could, the word would turn its head. In any case, it has something of an honest poetic space, of a page without a metaphor, a non-place without a place, with *another* place. What interested us is *poetry as exile*, which relates the topic to vagrancy, to nomadism. Exile is a primitive decentralization effect, a discovery of the margin before 'decentralization' and 'margin' were words, in a sociological, cultural, anthropological sense, successful in the hit-parades of truth, sadness, anger, and indigence. One imagines oneself in exile as in permanent movement. The imagination takes a place of privilege, an immediate participant in the expanding universe. This figure justifies the definition 'growing desert.' It suggests that the imagination accompanies it, goes with it. But the emptying or substitution of meaning is not what interests us: in most cases exile is an imposed punishment or the option of escaping to a punishment, to a sentence, to poverty. In exile one doesn't know if it's the wound or the pain that hurts. Did political exile anticipate the current waves of migration? Are we no longer born on a certain piece of land but rather in any place whatsoever under the stars? Exile is a place of coincidence, where the interior coincides with the exterior, what is inside with what is outside. When one asks a poem to be 'grounded' one asks of the poem the impossible: a root. Roots are what the poetic word does not have. 'It blooms because it blooms'; Angelis Silesius' lovely religious phrase with which Borges and José Ángel Valente define poetry means, among other things, 'rootless,' not from earth, more likely called down from heaven: 'lacking a reason,' and therefore having all of them, that is the 'reason' of the rose. 'Lacking a reason' is the same as 'rootless.' Generally the forgetting experienced in exile resembles a root that has been pulled up. In exile one is always already in exile, one doesn't arrive at it. One is there as if he or she had always been there. 'Shut in the Arcadia of the present,' says Antonio Machado. Doesn't the perpetual present tend to be the temporal illusion of a life sentence? The life sentence is not an illusion for the prisoner: it is a form of the greatest expressive humiliation, the mortal condition made eternal as a punishment. The blockade of the future, that machinery that hums along and doesn't move—or even seem to move—from one still point. Isn't it time that reigns over this system? Isn't this Promethean time? And here comes the foreseen question. Where is the eagle in all of this? The eagle stays in the heavens. And where are the heavens? Across the border. This is the only way I know to escape for a few moments the ever-present consciousness of exile—exile's prohibition seems to be to not forget: to join, not the justificatory order of the system, but to join in the game. This exercise in assonant rhythm seems more playful prose than documentation. Is that what it is? And those of us who had to leave for real, some through Brazil, others by a foreign embassy, others by the Montevideo International Airport? Choosing between eating shit or being dead? The state of the poetic word is analogous to the exilic state because of its rootless condition. Only that exile presupposes the human being. Except for metaphorically, the poetic word has not been exiled from any kingdom, any land, any country: at times, it was exiled from humanity. The word is not African, Australian, Asian: because it cannot be exiled. It is only poetic. The use of the poetic word does not presuppose an ethical commitment.

Chapter Three

Points of Discernment

It is impossible to approach certain problems relating to poetry without a global vision. Although it is true that poetry is a specific linguistic art, it requires a global vision. Poetry is a language that links things together. And it is so by contradiction: by being a specific language, for only the specific can speak in multiple ways. But it also requires, within the global vision, recognition of its specificity. Modernity taught us to view things globally, to see the totality on the margin of the nineteenth-century empires' attacks on the margin, so clearly modern in their Eurocentric vision. While our gazes were trained on modern globalism, imperial modernity concerned itself with strategic specificities. As a revulsive manifestation of this state of things, once the European spirit had gone into crisis, the aesthetico-historical Avant-Garde was the point on the lance of a global aesthetic vision: if it wasn't, what is the significance of the desire to implant a *koiné* or a language unique to art, a position located on the outskirts of the current babelization. But it's a difficult balance. The parcelling of existences that represent the different realities that currently make up the globalized world also requires that the specific gaze be situated: a view of specificity from a specific reality within the frame of a global context. Variability must be the condition for situating oneself in thought. The onslaught suffered by societies submerged in social and economic degradation may, in artistic practice, resent the weight of this punctually-arising historical baggage. There is no point in getting defensive. It's enough to know that it is so suicidal to stray from the global analysis that, though it may bring a negative charge to our particular reality, unavoidably, it amounts to self-negation as a community erased from history or as a desiring individuality. There is no shame in being part—which is not the same as agreeing with, let alone legitimizing—

of a predatory and dependent economy and being subject to a thinking existence that is immature. What is shameful is not rebelling against all of that. Globalization provides us with the alibi of forgetting our accumulated deficit of thought. Knowing ourselves to be immersed in a world with its own dynamic and an ideological package that guarantees that dynamic's immutability is a clear bill of health for our impotence. 'Going with the world' sounds less like a movement that expresses a shared dynamic than a consolation. More difficult is seeing the conditions in which we move through the immensity of that world. The flutter of a butterfly's wings in New York can precipitate a landslide in an Asian mountain. It's the hypothesis of interconnectedness. It's the victory of the minute over the monumental. And it's a physical metaphor for the interdependence of equilibriums. Or a warning about the movement of the oppressed and its effect on the stability of the oppressors. But it's cynical to consider beauty to be the obligatory result of putting up with any unjust order for the sake of the latent threat, always on the verge of becoming reality, that rebellion will cause widespread catastrophe. That approach to 'the end of history' is not feasible. It's valid only as an image, as a poetic effect. One has to consider the variants. The colloquial variant and its specificity, the fragmentary variant and its specificity, the variant of the Latin American view of poetry— and its specificities. And the semantic realm, will it return to hard-and-fast definitions, or will it poke its nose into nonsense? Fast answer: neither hard-and-fast definitions nor nonsense are the problem.

To speak of poetic colloquialism (spoken language, the language of the street) in poetry is not saying much in terms of a novel categorization: twentieth-century poetry is full of colloquial language. For anyone looking back from the future, colloquialism will define a good part of what has been done in contemporary poetry. And therefore, there is radical colloquialism and a colloquialism that understands poetry as the kind of language that 'tells it like it is,' and is, by that logic, 'true,' and equates such language with poetry. Poetic radicalism, however, does not distinguish between pure and colloquial language, between denotation and metaphor. Poetic radicalism depends on the state of poetry pertaining to an age, the state of poetic language at a given time. Only in this way does it make sense that Nicanor Parra's *anti-poetry* [antipoesía] can be seen as a radical poetic project that invokes other past radical, avant-garde poetics like Creationism and Surrealism. Without leaving Chile, in 1950, after Neruda's *Residence on Earth*, neither Creationism nor Surrealism have anything left to say. The reason is clear. Only as a negative approach to art, as a project that dissolves art into social practice, can the avant-garde be interpreted as a radical phenomenon. We have to uncover what's out in the open: full force at what is said and how it is said. Regrettably, the argument that venerates Parra bases itself on the first factor and not on the second. If *Poems and Anti-Poems* were not an investigation of spoken language, along the lines of an unmasking of a bad-tempered poetics and a bad-tempered poet, it would not have had the historic significance that it has. Radicalism is not only invention: it can be revealing the nakedness of the naked, pointing out what's there, which is often confused with the obvious. Without losing sight of the fact that colloquial poetic language, the one that famously 'speaks the way people speak,' celebrated because it 'tells the truth,' the 'marginal' language 'of the street corner,' is also a form of language whose only true effect lies in its mimesis of human speech outside of the poetic sphere and whose freshness is possible because of its greater ability to evade the norm. Considered in its canonical period—neoclassical language, for example, or even the poetic language of Baroque poetry in its historical moment—colloquial language, stuck to existence like a mollusk, insofar as it derives itself from it, expresses it, translates it, misrepresents it, reinvents it, is the ideal language for sabotaging dominant positions. There is an equation behind this very dear to post-Symbolist poetry: the identification of poetry with the sacred, non-poetry with existence. Life is non-poetic. The 'state' of poetry is opposed to 'life,' which translates itself through spoken language. A complete inversion: the 'pure and true' that confronts the 'corrupt' (in value) and the 'artificial' is precisely 'the millennial accumulation of all mistakes' (Oswald de Andrade), an excellent definition of colloquial language.

In *Razón de nadie* (Madrid: Ave del Paraíso, 1994) José-Miguel Ullán connects poetic colloquialism to a singular phase of alienation through a clear series of steps: 1. he considers it to be normative language; 2. he defines it as speech that is 'exterior' [*extraña*] to the person who speaks it; 3. he applies to colloquial language the same set of operations that would be applied to orthodox poetic language, that of a precise lexicon and usage: emptying of meaning, constant ellipsis, bleaching of iconicity— that is, a demonstration of its plasticity that tends to end up petrifying it as if it were any other language, robbing it of its fluidity and dynamism. This is, without a doubt, an *erasure of the colloquial* from the colloquial itself, which converts it into colloquial extract, stripped of the innumerable fillers that are its trademark. Ullán realized that, after taking the side of all that is not poetic in the poetic possibility of colloquial language, the only thing left to do was to extract it, to extradite it from itself. Once again, unmasking and invention:

DRY LEAF
Traditional
Its flight was not blue but I still remember that,
In that light, it appeared blue... (What
Should I focus on, tell me, if there's no hope
Nor net nor reverse nor appearance nor hardly
Anything
Like giving in to the undecided day
On which...)

[HOJA SECA
Tradicional
Su vuelo no era azul pero aún me acuerdo que,
acaso por la luz, lo parecía... (Y
a qué fijarse, di, si no hay remedio
ni red ni envés ni parecer ni casi
nada

> como el ceder al indeciso día
> en que...)]

The graceful cutting of the lines in this text adds an aftertaste of nostalgic disembodiment, an impossible *something more* that keeps itself, out of poetic fidelity, absent.

In *Levemente ondulado* (Montevideo, Arte Fatos, 2005), Roberto Appratto maintains a similar tone of skeletal colloquial speech:

> I sit down to write
> And keep silent. Through this act
> Of shutting at once my mouth
> And my thoughts
> I hear voices: I hear
> Some
> Voices
> That tell me what has been thought
> Regarding this topic.
>
> [Me siento a escribir
> y hago silencio. A partir de ese gesto
> de callarse la boca y al mismo tiempo
> el pensamiento
> escucho unas voces: escucho
> unas
> voces
> que dicen lo que se ha pensado
> al respecto.]

This is something quite different from the colloquial poetics that are practiced today, for example, in Argentina. The 'this-is-not-poetry' alibi makes verbal experiences derived too closely from experience worth something. As 'spoken experiences' of little depth, language cannot be objectified; it is impossible to work with it. Poetry's confidence rests on the fact that it works with a living and lived language. The question is: since when and to what extent? The 'for whom' is understood. An egalitarian of colloquialism like Washington Cucurto in *Hatuchay* (México, El Billar de Lucrecia, 2005) would reply, 'For the neighborhood.' Which means, roughly, 'for people like me,' 'for those who live in these circumstances.' One must not forget that the neighborhood, as a sentimental location, is to ever-shifting, global exile what family is to the State, the kind of whispered rumor that Nésto Perlongher criticized so well in 'Cadáveres' with the expression 'esto no sale de aquí' [in Spanish, both 'this doesn't come from here' and 'this doesn't leave the room']. And one of the undeniable tasks of poetry is, precisely this in both senses of the Spanish: belonging to this place, coming from here, and the opposite action: going away. All at once: coming from a place in order to leave that place. Exile everywhere.

To say 'fragment' in relation to poetic writing is not saying much, literally. In general, of course, fragment is understood as brevity, in terms of the amount of expression: the fragment is a brief thing just as art is a *cosa mentale*, almost by leonardesque imperative. And it is not necessarily so. The fragment is discontinuity, interruption, remnant, hollow, hole, extract, part. And the written mimesis of something outside: the universe in expansion, for example. And of something above, Mallarmé's constellation. Writing that is here for what is not here, would be an approximate definition. But the fragment quarrels with definition. Always, and especially in these times: incompleteness. With the following ambiguity: one does not know whether it doesn't reach completeness or if it ceased to exist, if it's coming or going. What remains between two absences. Mimesis once again, this time of life. A Deleuzian phrase: 'what is in between,' *entre*. Writing in fragments seems like an act of freedom. Just read Beckett, Jabès, Leopardi, Ungaretti, several of the Avant-Garde masters, César Vallejo's *Trilce* (1922)—an historic date that certainly does represent a *since when*—Antonio Gamoneda, Olvido García Valdés, and recently, Marcos Canteli. But it is an act of stringent restriction:

>   Now minute-counting ants
>   Go in sweetened, sleepy, scarcely
>   Disposed, and they pile up,
>   Burned dust, as high as
>   (Vallejo, *Trilce*, 1921)

> [Ahora hormigas minuteras
> se adentran dulzoradas, dormitadas, apenas
> dispuestas, y se baldan,
> quedamadas pólvoras, altos de a
>   (Vallejo, *Trilce*), 1921]

> I saw lavender blossoms submerged in a bowl of weeping and
> the vision burned within me,
>   (Gamoneda, *Arden las pérdidas*)

> [Vi lavandas sumergidas en un cunco de llanto y la visión ardió
> en mí]
>   (Gamoneda, *Arden las pérdidas*)]

> he doesn't have the gift of eloquence, words don't come easy,
> proper nouns escape him the moment he tries to use them, often
> regular nouns evade him, too
>   the word flees through a hole
>   paralyzed for an instant it contemplates that hole
>   the missing word shows him the way by which he loses
> himself, in the direction of the dead, of / the non-self
>   (García Valdés, *Libro de los líquenes o el decir*)

[carece del don de la elocuencia, no tiene facilidad de palabra,
se le escapan los nombres propios en el momento en que va a
utilizarlos, con frecuencia también le faltan los comunes
   la palabra huye por un agujero
       paralizada por un instante contempla ese agujero
           la palabra que falta le señala el lugar por el que se pierde,
dirección de lo muerto, del no-yo
   (García Valdés, *Libro de los líquenes o el decir*)]

the words would like
a fishing line—*and that one,*
who burned him? for it's burning me

        (Canteli, *Su sombrío*)

[quisieran tanza
las palabras —*¿y aquél*
quién lo quemó? que a mí me quema

        (Canteli, *Su sombrío*)]

Notice the difference in the disposition of the quoted writing in the cases of Ullán and Appratto, on the one hand, texts broken up by commentary when addressing the theme of poetic colloquialism, and the texts that follow, where the question of the fragment is taken up, sequential and contiguous quotations separated by the credit to the author and the title of the book. The citations of author and title break up the unity of the fragment, a good demonstration of a 'fragmentary vertical axis,' almost a palimpsest.

One has to *come after* in order to write fragmentarily. One has to have gone through an agonic phase in poetic writing (the Avant-Garde in the historical meaning of frontier or limit: not as a museographic fragilization of art, a glasswork that ultimately crystallized at room temperature), in society (the toppling of an earlier order, the failure of substitution, an aborted or incomplete metaphor), or as an individual (a crisis upon facing death, for example). This last produced the best book of Latin American poetry in the last quarter-century: *Hospital británico* (1986) by Héctor Viel Temperley. A book constructed from precise amounts of intensity can only be written fragmentarily. Another characteristic of the fragment: intensity. Viel Temperley says:

Rosetto Pavilion, the long corner of summer, framework of
    butterflies: My mother came to see me in heaven.

My head is bandaged. I remain in the breast of
Light for hours and hours. I am happy. They have taken
me out of the world.

My mother is laughter, freedom, summer.

Twenty blocks away, she lies dying.

Here she kisses my peace, sees her son changed, and prepares
herself
—in Your weeping—to start everything over again

[Pabellón Rosetto, larga esquina de verano, armadura de
mariposas: Mi madre vino al cielo a visitarme.

Tengo la cabeza vendada. Permanezco en el pecho de la
Luz horas y horas. Soy feliz. Me han sacado del
mundo.

Mi madre es la risa, la libertad, el verano.

A veinte cuadras de aquí yace muriéndose.

Aquí besa mi paz, ve a su hijo cambiado, se prepara
—en Tu llanto— para comenzar todo de nuevo]

This is one of the few texts in more-or-less recent Latin American poetic writing that resemble lasting—if not eternal—work, work that will triumph—that is what the shock caused by this text communicates: something declares in advance that it will conquer time, according, of course, to our ever shrinking possibilities of sustainability—time within an artistic operation that is situated outside of time: the art of this age does not conquer time. It falls victim to its own precariousness as a sign of triumph, negative power, or disdain for the impossible. Something of Zurita's also resembles lasting work: *Purgatorio* (1979). And on the opposite side, something by Diego Maquieira that acts as a counterdance to this counterpoint, a post-epic epic to make the epic impossible in case it tries to propagate its heaviness, its repetition rendered unbelievable: *Los Sea Harrier* (1993). Against the grain of both of these, for its clear, long-term effect in the formal response to radicalism more than for its schizo-mesmerizing abilities, the masterwork of the second half of the twentieth century in poetry and in Latin America: *La nueva novela* (1985) by Juan Luis Martínez. There is a *suffering for the text* on the part of the reader of Viel Temperley's poem that captures the attempt at *suspension* (the space of poetic dignity) in which the text is situated as a transcendence of the temporal sustained by individual suffering. That space of *suspension* is delimited in such a way that it restricts implication to any context not indexed by the text itself: minimal contextualization, a historicity that is at odds with dates—no text in twentieth-century Latin American lyric is more dated—individual helplessness at odds with the imposition of history that accepts the date insofar as it dates itself in recognition of its—momentary—unrepeatable condition. Jacques Derrida considers this when paying homage to Paul Celan in *Shibboleth* (1986), which is a great homage to Paul Celan and among the best of Jacques Derrida's devotional writing. One of those books of which the reader says, 'That's how a book should be written,' as if the book had not yet been written, as if the imperative were to write it sometime, at some point in time, unequivocal proof of the triumph of writing: when it generates its own desire to be written within the reader, in order, as Viel Temperley says, 'to start everything over again.'

Translated by Leslie Harkema

Parra and Concrete Poetry

For Edgardo Dobry

The relationship between Nicanor Parra and Brazilian Concrete Poetry holds within it the possibility of sketching out the current parameters of writing. Other occurrences of a poetic nature during the years that concern us here are the publication of *La insurrección solitaria* [The Solitary Insurrection] by Carlos Martínez Rivas (1953) and *En la masmédula* [In the Moremarrow] by Oliverio Girondo (1954).

The appearance, a true historic epiphany—let the contradiction stand—of *Poemas y antipoemas* [*Poems and Antipoems*] by Nicanor Parra in 1954 transformed Latin American poetry from the Castilian side. This distinction is important: in Latin America everything seems to be Castilian when it is not; not everything is Iberian, although we discovered this late. We have moved from a double poetic influence, the Castilian and the French, to a double geographical-poetic ring: Brazilian poetry to the South, North American poetry to the North. What Parra breaks from, among other things, is Latin American poetry's dependence upon that double influence, more traditional than contemporary. Parra comes from an amalgam of traditions: in him there are traces of the Portuguese Alberto Caeiro (Fernando Pessoa), there are traces of the medieval romances, there is also the imprint of Villon. But above all there is a great deal of Anglo-Saxon poetics introduced by virtue of epistemology: the belief that the word is the thing, without regard for the arbitrary relationship between thing and sign. If credence is given to this last statement, what reaches the common reader is not language, and especially not poetic language. And in Parra what gets broken, the other thing that Parra breaks away from is the dependence upon an understanding of poetry as related to an elite reader, a specialized language for specialized eyes. The perverse inheritance of the avant-garde—which wanted to dissolve art in social praxis, according to Peter Bürger—was that poetry ended up as the cult object of consumers who returned to the nineteenth century, to a decadent dandyism, long before the poets, who returned afterwards; that is, today. The reader of poetry preceded the poet in this return by fifty years—if the reader of poetry had ever left the nineteenth century in the first place. Another thing broken by Parra is the *auratic* condition of the poet, which originated, in that Chilean moment, directly from Pablo Neruda. An aside: in 1950 Neruda had already renounced his most radical work, *Residencia en la Tierra* [Residence on Earth] 1 and 2. In *Tercera residencia* [Third Residence], in the fragment 'Explico algunas cosas' [I'll Explain a Few Things] from the section 'España en el corazón' [Spain In the Heart], he says the following of that radical stage, which is almost a poetic slip for Neruda: 'You will ask: And where are the lilies / And the metaphysics covered with poppies?' In this astonishing metaphor, the most condensed self-criticism that I've seen in a poetic work, Neruda, taking the path of 'realist poetry' (as he calls it), managed to deal with one of the most intense moments of Latin American poetry at any time. He dealt with its incommunicable phase, not with its aura. Neruda continued believing, and many with him, in the vatic character of the poet. *Canto general* [General Song] is a great vaticination. That which spoke with the abyss will attempt a dialogue with the people, and, in their name, with history without losing even the smallest shimmer of the aura. Out of this mythopoetic context, somewhere between historic and so deliriously subjective that it no longer complies with its historic importance (the nineteenth-century poet-vaticinator played on two fronts: the consolation of the bourgeois conscience even through aggression, and the withdrawal from society to the point of disappearance; Rimbaud passed through both phases) comes Nicanor Parra. It is evident that the first thing one must understand, in dealing with Parra, is the local conception of poetry as equivalent to the linguistic production of an unleashed imaginary. The confusion that equates image with poetry, or even more radical and difficult, metaphor with poetry, was a dominant constant in Latin American poetics at the middle of the last century. The first equation is a product of Surrealism and the second of the Spanish Golden Age that came in through the door or the window of exile during the Franco dictatorship. When I say image and metaphor I am speaking of tropological levels and of resources that come from a rhetorical-literary apparatus. I refer here to an identification that attempts to be substantial, and not merely a juncture for a choice of poetics. I refer here to a true metaphysics of resources—let the contradiction stand—whose only possibility of being destroyed lies in a retreat of language from its own rhetoric. It is as if Nicanor Parra had taken the linguistic table cloth out from under the resources and the Nerudian artifice was seen for what it really was: just another rhetorical apparatus that talks to itself, reciting its monologue to a captive audience. It is interesting to point out that the abundance of images and metaphors, the proliferation of tropological resources, does not imply that the poem will open to an *outside*. On the contrary, they can contribute—and generally this is what happens—to a tropological self-absorption that the reader is inclined to accept as *what really is*. I call this 'the captive reader': the reader who obeys the identification of poetry with a series of resources and doesn't recognize it when those resources are absent. We could say that the true opening of the poem to the *outside* is only possible when the poem reveals its constitutive mechanisms. Paul de Man calls this *irony*, after Walter Benjamin. A poem by Nicanor Parra from *Poems and Antipoems* acts as a key to that book and to what I am saying: 'Advertencia al lector' [Warning to the Reader]. Throughout the entire text Parra speaks to the reader from *outside* the poem: 'According to the teachers of the law, this book should not be published,' etc. At the end of the text he re-enters the textual *inside*. How? By way of a metaphor: 'Aristophanes's birds / buried in their own heads / the cadavers of their fathers / (Each bird was a bona-fide flying cemetery.)' Here we must note that the metaphor appears by way of a double operation: the first, a fairly logical, not poetic, part occurs as a synthesis of the explanatory process according to the 'if… then…' model. We can call this method, parodying the Brazilian critic Joao Aleixandre Barbosa, a 'critical metaphor.'

The other is dazzlingly absurd: if the first proposition is true, as a product of a completely mythical, irrational civil-imaginary context, the second proposition is delirious. I fear that here Nicanor Parra believed that metaphor was the delirium that succeeded in separating poetry from common mortals. But this metaphorical operation is critical for one reason: the metaphor does not present itself without explanation but rather appears in the text by way of deduction. If Parra as speaker had addressed the reader from outside the poem throughout the whole text he could have not reentered the poem in any way other than through an external operation, through a logic that is external to poetry even if the trope is—according to a very Castilian view, of course—considered the equivalent of poetry itself.

The reception of this text is still surprising. It varies between being taken for a certain predictability in the logic of canonical anti-methods and the denial of its status as a poetic text at all. Indeed, it is considered to be a text *outside of poetry*. In this negative reading a crucial fact is often overlooked: contemporary post-avant-garde poetry is a kind of poetry that is, indeed, *outside of poetry* and within a historical process in art in general that begins in the nineteenth century with the reflections of German idealism and with the punctual thought of Hegel and Schlegel. It is important for me to restore the relevance to this question of process in which contemporary poetry enters, not out of obedience to history but as resistance to the historical counterblow that views as 'bad moments' in Western art both the nineteenth-century thought regarding the disintegration of art and the dissolutive proposals of the aesthetic-historic avant-gardes at the beginning of the last century. It would be very difficult to conceive of Rimbaud, Mallarmé, or Laforgue and Corbière without the first of these 'bad moments.' Without the second, it is impossible to conceive of Nicanor Parra, Oliverio Girondo, Carlos Martínez Rivas, or Concrete Poetry; not forgetting, of course, Vallejo, Oswald de Andrade, Huidobro, Neruda, Westphalen.

It is likely that in Latin America the most intense 'bad moment' we have, although situated within the Portuguese language and its Brazilian variation, is the Concrete Poetry movement, created in Sao Paulo in 1952 by poets Augusto and Haroldo de Campos and Décio Pignatari. In their 'war period'—that's what they call it—that stretches into the sixties, the concrete poets propose a re-evaluation of the aesthetic-historical avant-gardes with an adjustments to the historical situation at mid-century. What is devastatingly clear in the Concrete Poets is the following: the historical avant-gardes—Dadaism, Soviet Futurism, Constructivism, North American Modernism (never Surrealism, which they critique because they don't consider Surrealism to be an avant-garde endeavor)—have run their course by 1952. But they have left a formal legacy that, always within the *presentifying* logic that the concrete poets took from Ezra Pound, can be used in the present separately from the revolutionary attitude and impetus of the historic avant-gardes. Here a strange and contradictory phenomenon occurs: upon acknowledging the present validity of the formal repertory of the aesthetic-historic avant-gardes apart from their attitude that first governed this repertory historically, the concrete poets, for the first time in Latin America, are dividing a historical fusion: that of a new art and a new man. The fact that the synthesis of these two, as Peter Bürger says, was the attempt to dissolve art in social praxis speaks eloquently to this. So that now the revolutionary character of early twentieth-century avant-garde radicalism must be absorbed by the creation of a radical poetic form. The world may not change, but poetry can. The idea of a 'synthetic-ideographic' poem, made up of 'piths and gists,' the integration of the verbal-vocal-visual triad (semantic, oral, plastic or iconic) that makes up every poem since Mallarmé's *Un coup de dés* (1897) still owes much to the bourgeois conception of the poem as an 'art object,' and much more to the poetic specter that haunts the mass-produced object of the nineteenth century's Industrial Revolution, where that very object, paradoxically, is placed in crisis by Mallarmé. It is true that the logic of the Mallarméan poem, the absolute talisman or totem of twentieth-century experimental poetry, presents an equal amount of constructive and deconstructive strokes, depending on the angle from which it is viewed. Concrete Poetry restores a positivity to Mallarmé's poem in the same way that Octavio Paz does so. See the epilogue to the second edition of *El arco y la lira* [The Bow and the Lyre] (1967), 'Los signos en rotación' [Rotating Signs], a true exaltation of Mallarmé's poem, holding it to be the undeniable touchstone for twentieth-century poetic art. It is strange, I insist, how both the concrete poets and Paz declare the end of the negative phase of modern art by invoking one of modern art's sharpest critics in the nineteenth century: Mallarmé. It is valid to ask on what point of affirmation they base themselves in order to achieve this synthesis. That point of affirmation is clearly not to be found in Europe (in this regard we can see T. S. Eliot's *The Waste Land*, published the same year as Vallejo's *Trilce* and James Joyce's *Ulysses*, 1922, where Eliot already reveals what he sees as the true meaning of the rupture proposed by the avant-garde—a collapse that is not only artistic-aesthetic but also civil—and makes the calm water of nostalgia for myth flow beneath the choppy waters of poetic form). The point of affirmation is found in North American poetry, the poetry of a country that resolved the contradiction with the actual elimination of its historical past. With one base in Mallarmé and another in Pound, cummings, and Williams, the Concrete Poets managed to come out well in the area of proposing a synthetic-positive, completely functional art object that fulfills its technological role at its particular moment in history. Undoubtedly, it could be said that Surrealism and even Dada could have occurred as movements while it was still the nineteenth century. Concrete Poetry could not. Already here we have an unequivocal demarcation of an aesthetic field and of a location of conditions for the object's utility in the area of poetry. The extreme restriction of the characteristics of the concrete poem according to the *lowest-common-multiple* logic of language allows for a savings that belies all of that George-Bataille-philosophical-French lust that situated poetry within the notion of unproductivity and sheer waste. The truth is also this: from a formal point of view, from the formal view of the poem, Concrete Poetry does not constitute a critique of the capitalist system of production, with the exception of Décio

Pignatari's contribution of a semantic prosecution of the poem in two instances, examples of true iconic resistance: 'Terra' from 1956 and 'Beba Coca-Cola' [Drink Coca-Cola] from 1957. In its most intense period—the truly 'concrete' period, as it were—Concrete Poetry is a historically situated poetry—that is, having a place and a function. What it represents—and this is a lot for a continent like Latin America, which has not managed to think seriously in terms of a new art, whatever that might be in the historical present—is a rigorous and consistent example for demonstrating, from a local, anthropological-cultural invocation, the urgent need for a new conception of the poem halfway through the last century. The Concrete Poets point to, within their framework of influences, the poet-thinker behind the Modern Art Week in 1922, Oswald de Andrade, whose Cannibal Manifesto, written six years later, is of a reflective actuality that is at least intriguing, as if the time of Latin American critical reflection had frozen and, from time to time, thawed inopportunely, only to return again to a steady state of non-thought. In the case of Concrete Poetry, this is not just an attempt to synthesize the legacy formally disseminated by the historical avant-gardes. It is also, like Nicanor Parra's antipoems, an attempt to contain a poetic—and practical—vision that would later prove itself to be uncontainable: that of a poetry that returns to a psuedo-auratic subjective space where any aesthetic conception is valid, any form accepted and any body of semantic signification pre-emptively legitimated. Strangely, a poetics of colloquial language directed to the common man and a poetics that presents itself as a synthetic distillation of Western poetic form, as Concrete Poetics does, have the same enemy: the reader and producer of a kind of poetic language that presents itself as ahistorical, whose only notion of subjectivity is the intersection between sentimental confessionalism and off-key practice of a kind of formalization that considers itself to be extratemporal. This producer-reader, whom I call the enemy for merely operative reasons, would try to mediate, would try to make of itself a third way between two proposals that are, for different reasons, radical. But he cannot, for one simple reason. In this reader-producer there is no assimilation of the problematics uncovered by both Parra and the Concrete Poets. For this reader-producer poetry is still essentially the same, 'nothing has changed' in the realm of art and of poetic art. Art and poetry count on the aid of a system, contemporary imperial capitalism, that imposes a devastating reality on a third of the world's population and an uncritical, anaesthetized way of life on the rest of the population. The dream of that false mediation is just that: a dream from which the current system and the producers of poetry of accompaniment (for that is how it can be characterized: poetry for going to the movies, poetry for after dinner) do not need nor want to wake up. Real poetic resistance with its eyes on a possible transformation occurred during the past mid-century, one foot in Spanish-speaking Latin America, another in Portuguese-speaking Latin America. What we are living through now, I'd like to believe momentarily, is the triumph of an agreed-upon reception: a lot of artistic practice, a lot of art objects, little or no thought. And already a long time ago, since the middle of the twentieth century, approximately, customary poetic production strangely coincides with its reception.

Translated by Leslie Harkema

3

TO WRITE ABOUT WRITING POETRY

1. To write about *writing poetry* implies thinking about suspension, among other things that occur under a condition of discontinuity. There is a decision made slowly, daily, so that it becomes impossible to discover the moment of detonation that might have announced, in another, more certain time, the budding of a destiny. The starting point was lost in time. To discover the moment of initiation as if it could be staged—the chair there; the table, the books, and the photos in the back; above, the night, the stars—is to parody Mallarmé at just the right moment: the moment when he would dress himself to write.

Other types of writing allow one to go looking for the facts—a novelist takes many notes, consults carpentry manuals, dictionaries of plants, dictionaries of birds, atlases, annuals, almanacs, and personal calendars—the ones used to remember birthdays. An essayist carries out excavations, at the slightest provocation he grabs a spade and starts to dig: the essay has a lot in common with poetry.

It is tempting to think that the act of writing poetry has not changed much over time. The same reasoning leads to the assertion that poetry *is always the same*. This notion—the conviction of some practitioners who see in poetry the reflection of their own need to endure—becomes muddied especially when one faces the reality of poetry in this historical moment. If it is true that poetry has turned various circles around itself since the (Hegelian, nineteenth-century) *death of art*—the philosophical foundation of the emergence of the aesthetic-historic avant-gardes of the first decades of the twentieth century—and if it is also true that it has rejected that symbolic 'death' and returned to the classical resources of versification, clear and hard facades, and specific themes (three moments that synthesize the instant of splendor in the avant-garde's rejection of any idea of poetic tradition), its reality has changed in terms of the various conceptions of its practice that currently exist. Today an eternalist vision, untouched by the fire of daily life but very touched by the fire of the gods upon whose continued presence, up there in some corner of the ether, this eternalist vision places its wager, coexists with 'vehicular' notions of poetry: one, that which communicates the needs of a specific community; another, that which uses the poetic word as an instrument of persuasion or to enable consciences for a change in society. All of them taking a nihilistic view with regard to their influence on the receptor: nothing can modify the indifference of the human being at present, neither the soul in the quill of Guido Cavalcanti nor the most arid and wild João Cabral de Melo Neto, the Brazilian Cavalcanti. Between the contemporary of Dante and the integrator of the Generation of 1945 in Brazilian literature a lot of poetic water has flowed past, subterranean at times, streams of water most times, sprinkling the critical gaze with a blurry oscillation between passion and unease. But what matters here, right now, is signification, the act of writing poetry considered as a phenomenon in itself. I have my doubts as to whether a precise vision of poetry carries with it a way of writing (not merely a technique, note merely handwritten or typed). We have to find that way of writing neither *for* nor *in absence of*, we have to recuperate the mode of writing *just because*, attentive to any outside world: that of the old Chinese man of the Tang dynasty who watches the leaves fall in the time of the eyes of the beloved who is not there; that of Mallarmé when he conquered the blankness of the page with a pure stare in order to set himself up on the precipices of an abyss with the noise of water and wings against the sky; that of today, here. A way of writing attentive to the voracities of every world that jumps, speaks, shouts, breaks, annihilates, ventures out, conspires, descends a pine-lined street united with the lovers under the pines: everything that reveals our fragility and our impotence before things. And even more— this is important—a way of writing attentive to the weight of the word, the mental weight that hangs in the shade and builds on its own. And finally: to write poetry is the only way I know of to believe in the existence of a listener for the word or, if there are none anymore, to precipitate the moment of their creation: the creation of the birth of a listener. Not what the scholars mean when they say 'every writer creates his reader': the creation of the birth of a listener so that a world, now unheard-of because it has been forgotten, the world of *attention*, might be born.

2. One creates the spectres of one's lineage, or their spectral way of appearing. Why did I always feel tied to Guillaume de Poitiers and his 'Farey un vers de dreyt nien' [I made a poem of nothing]? Because that's how a poem is made: so many grams of love from the hole left by love's body, plus so many grams of flour to make bread dampened by the rain that fell through the split beams, create that kind of a dream that gives itself over to a paradise at the moment of the disintegration of an entire age: after lunch at midday, half asleep above the rhythm of the horse's footfalls one moves under the leaves, at the edge of the cool shade, following the stone wall. Given over to this certainty: it could have been different or not have been at all. This poem might not have been, nor any leaves to shade the horse's steps, nor any Guillame de Poitiers, retired to the natural light of his castle to write any words about those yellow leaves, crackling like cheese in a fire, dehydrated of any poison and poisonous plant, not even at nighttime by the pale light of a candelabra. It might not have been. To write is then to take the chance that consciousness will tolerate the possibility of 'it might not have been' immediately after it really was: a remainder, a balance, a surplus of the action that took shape. That makes us—art's head circles around the mundane ocean of things, notes, news, devastated Palestine children—less pure, more real, with the notion of humanity half lost in these lands.

Translated by Leslie Harkema

Key Words
A Few Words to Defend,
Not Everything Can Be Negotiated

CHANCE

The first and only opening word would be 'chance'. That word defined my life; I don't know if once or twice. It is a word very much wedged into my existence, twice wedged: in orphanhood and in transgression, in the death of my mother and in the imprisonment of my father. Of course, Mallarmé's great poem springs to mind: *Un coup de dés jamais n'abolira le hasard*, a poem where chance gambles with form. So I would say that in my unconscious reading of this poem they get played, every time I read it, these two instances of my life, these two *chances*. Nothingness is so present that it offers itself as refuge. As if the words 'here pass those who don't have', 'those who have nothing', had been written across its non-existent doorway. One should not forget that this poem is an emblem of modernity; that it marks the fulfilment of a cycle, the exhaustion of a ritual; an exhaustion foreseen by Baudelaire. The other day I was telling Philippe[1] that French poetry had taken over modernity in the nineteenth century; particularly by signalling the fulfilment, by evidencing, the cycle of exhaustion. It is a ritual that ends in Nothingness. French poetry completed the narrative of exhaustion. It took the game to its final consequences. From a different side, in the same century, a new literature arose virtually 'out of nowhere'; it arose, it did not end there: North American Literature. A literature that began inventing everything, as if there weren't a past to close down. It is the other face of this Nothingness, a Nietzschean face, a face of a *tabula rasa*: 'from this point forward', not 'up to this point'; an opening rather than a closure. It could be said that French poetry compels to change, but North American poetry compels to give birth.

---
[1] Philippe Ollé-Laprune (France, 1962).

How it is born, on top of what, it's another matter. Baudrillard reminds us the feeling of desolation, of utter desolation, that nature in North American evokes on us (I won't say the United States because I'm still talking about the nineteenth century), underpinned by the extermination of Native Americans; if you compare it to what happened in Latin America, it was the great majority of them, almost a complete extermination. However, what distinguishes both sides of the limit is not the struggle between depletion and youth, it is memory. French poetry does not want to lose its memory, perhaps because it can't. France invents the final stretch of modernity, an enlightened stretch, the moment before the confusion we find ourselves in now. As much as Rimbaud attempts to escape with the scar of a bullet in his body, and Mallarmé attempts ritualistically to dissolve himself into Nothingness as a mode of purification—he had lost his son, Anatole—neither poet can escape the capacity to remember. North America wanted to erase memory by precisely erasing what was autochthonous, what's from there, its native people. They wanted to keep the place without its people. It's curious that one of the strands of North American poetry, a strand of great fertility, as it were, not for its depth but rather for its overflowing, its ambitiousness, its conquering spirit, is Whitman's. That is, poetry seen as a world, as world of things to be precise. Let's not forget that we're in the nineteenth century, in the heyday of the Industrial Revolution, amid the explosions of industrial production, literally of steam in the wind. We hare here in the era of the world as a thing, the prelude to the human coldness that we live in now. First is the reification of the world; first come the things, then the coldness.

EXILE

A lot has been said about literature from the lens of modernity. Among other things, it has been said that literature is an act of exile; the exiled writer, the exiled page. Today we might think of it as a sort of transhumance. But we are now in a certain modern twilight that is often confused, like Nothingness, with a dawn. But the prestige of exile is a modern concern, an effect of dislocation, a scattering of people, a continuous repopulation. People leave their place of origin. This is important: there is no defining origin. The wanderer is a man who repeats an ancient nomadic condition. This that happens now after the crisis of modernity: the transient man, the man without a fixed place. The page becomes an abode for this man, which is also temporary. The equivalency of page with place rotates: the page becomes the space where the poetic sign passes thorough, a metaphor of space where man passes through. Thus every sign is transitory. However, what would be important is that things would not be this way, and not the legitimization of this circumstance. Place matters, it is given by the mother, the mother and everything she implies, man's topological bond. Poetic form has clearly to do with this. It has been dispersed since Mallarmé. The imagination of a rotating cosmos matters—the signs, I'm thinking of Octavio Paz here. And man was going to rotate, as before he ploughed the earth. Without a place, man rotates, woman rotates, and they plough everything. How could we not have anticipated this? With this landscape there are no possible bonds, and if no bonds are possible, there is no possibility for transcendence; the pivot to move the world. What is a possible pivot now? We have to imagine a world that does not depend on a single pivot. We must constantly be renewing these. Writing should keep a record all of this. In Latin America writers prefer to write outside of time, as if they were saying, outside of all of this. The consciousness that exile gives prevents the practice of sedentary writing; a too sedentary one. The impression I get from this sedentary writing is that it belongs to a man from an ancient past, who does not live among us anymore, and whose antiquity, like a projection, cannot reach us. However, I recognize the nostalgia for stability, for a land, for a bond, for a formal work. I venture the following: one cannot renounce form. I would almost say that a certain guarantee—which matters to everyone—of poetic effectiveness consists in disguising nostalgia at a time when the new is constantly being disguised. Or is it time itself disguised in order to give the appearance of the new? Something strange is happening here, time and the new are coexisting. When we think of modern exile, we shouldn't forget something important. In general when we speak of exile, we speak of it in terms of exile before exile and exile after exile, but not of exile as movement. What I can say about this is the following: your can never leave exile behind. There is forgetfulness, but you cannot leave it behind. Except for those who believe in some kind of return.

FRAGMENT

This is what writing is. Writing is more or less fragmentary but it cannot escape the fragment. The fragment is a testimony in itself. It testifies the whole as a part. It's a detachment, an expression that I like because it defines the fragment. Then, or before, it is a breaking free, a breaking free from those damned captors in these lands of captors. The word capture is one of the terrible words of our time. Everything is captured, from information to human beings, to human organs. To make matters worse, the verb presupposes an escape, a freedom that, with each act performed, with each capture, is annulled and sealed off as freedom. This is one of the words that reveals where and how we are now. And half of humanity is happy to use it. Again, the fragment is the image of a detachment that had negative connotations insofar as it abandoned a belonging; it became detached. The fragment makes detachment positive. It remembers the part and continues on without it. The fragment, and not the foot, invents the footprint. A prisoner is someone who is held. Likewise, life is held to the world with pins. This we already know about. Pin in Spanish is *alfiler*, an Arabic word.

CRITICISM

Criticism is a concept relative to thought. It is not in life. But it is altogether representative of that articulation of thought we call modernity. Criticism as available matter for thought but also as an act that belongs to it, this is rooted in the Enlightenment. Post-Enlightenment modernity has the obligation—I repeat, the obligation, not the right nor the possibility—to think critically. Somehow to dare to think for one self which stems from Kant. Criticism among us is a notion of philosophical order displaced into culture and society. It isn't a practice; people do not think, or act, or live critically. There is fear. This fear comes from different directions. It certainly comes from institutions of the establishment, from beyond institutions and before institutes, and from institutions from the beyond. All of this produces fear. This fear that is taught is a fear of criticism as a dissolving act. Only what is solid can be dissolved. This, since the Communist Manifesto, has been stated clearly and in writing, from a time when dialectics still existed in our thinking. Otherwise it cannot be formulated. The panic in the guardians of the 'solid' over pseudo-dissolving agents draws attention. From this point of view, criticism is outside, on the other side of solids. Its presence is a threat. Why is it that in certain cultures, in certain countries, criticism has not been able to be perceived as a constituent element of solidity, shall we say, as what increases and constitutes solidity? At this moment it is extremely rare to find truly critical thinking. First because the moment of critical thinking seems to have ended with the century that has just ended. This last thought works as long as our disproportionate trust in the idea of century allows us to believe that with the end of the century it also ended a world, a mode of thinking, and, perhaps, a man. But that world, those men, and that thinking were bearers of reality. How did they manage to pass through and leave us to resolve all the aggravated problems? Adorno wrote about criticism that '[it] does no harm because it dissolves… but to the extent that it obeys the forms of rebellion.' Isn't this an X-ray of the moment we are living now? The problem then isn't about dissolution, but about complicity, about the legitimizing by means of pseudo-criticism. For a long time we claimed we were victims of the media, as spectators, as passive bodies. As if the media would have had the power of criticism on their side, something that has never happened. The relationship with media is one of dependency rather than submission. Which is worse, of course; it's difficult to rebel against one's own dependency.

POEM

It is a kind of 'occimoron', not an oxymoron, the relationship between two antagonistic elements, not the 'Moor in the Occident', but rather, an Occidental moratorium. Poetry is a delayed act. A poem is precise but belated. It arrives late because there is nowhere to come to. It is unfinished. It is always not finishing. Even if it finishes, it continues. Without a doubt, as the great Paulo Leminski says, it is the territory of freedom; one of the few. Those who write know that from a poem's pores comes air one can breathe. That, for the moment, is freedom. Later, we will see. This is about the freedom in a poem; the freedom to make. I don't know where else it might happen, but there, in the territory of the poem, freedom rises up there while one is making it. And if it is well made the poem maintains the effect of freedom rising up. There are many ways to talk about a poem in relation to what *is being*. It is an act where a man becomes aware of his dimension, not of another's. The word 'size' is pornographic or financial. If for a moment it ever to be that, I would say that in writing a poem a man becomes aware of his size. What happens when he reads a poem written by someone else? He becomes aware of both, the author's size and his own; the poem levels.

POLITICS

We are in trouble. It seems that the pretended relationship between people within the *polis* has been completely discredited. It's not an etymological problem. It's impossible to escape the city. Politics continues in the country, it reaches into the jungle. Militant political action can be an ennobling action: the quality of life changes, very favorably in some cases. Above all when we struggle for a transformation with full awareness that it is about transformation for the better, within this awareness. The discredit in our countries has been complete. Political action is a manifestation of a class, a political class, and rarely a manifestation of a community, what once was called the people. The full charge, the entire weight of the political class revolves around a pseudo-administration where the whole extent of its political interests comes into play. In some countries the politician, the professional politician, has become synonymous with disrepute. This fact is truly dire. And one cannot, for the sake of precisely political honesty, take shelter in a Western pseudo-mythopoetics, and respond to the current political catastrophe from across the road, on a poetic side, as if there were, I insist, an advantage, something else that lived outside the walls of the city. As Virilio says, the borders are no longer outside of the city, they're inside, everything bordering everything else, with muddled edges. The discrediting of politics, or of the political class identified with political action, is extremely grave. If we lose that trust we fall on the hands, it would seem, of complete uncertainty. We would have to ask ourselves, pragmatically, whether this is for the better or for the worse. At any rate, if we ask ourselves who benefits from the discrediting of the political class, the answer is: that same political class that is now free to carry out its political project. Or is it conceivable that behind the discrediting of the political class there isn't a political project of reversibility of that order of things?

CONCRETENESS

I never wrote concrete poetry. But I learned a great deal from the concrete poets of Sao Paulo: Augusto and Haroldo de Campos and Décio Pignatari. I am still grateful for the clarity of those poets, for having had access to that clarity, and for having personally known those three greats of Latin American poetry. It seems incredible that we should have first had to cross the threshold of concrete poetry in order to realize that all poetry is a phenomenon of the concreteness of poetic language. The opposite is that vagueness, that imprecision with which most of the lyrical West has delighted us. Let's suppose that certain precepts of concrete poetry are now more debatable than they were in the 1950s, at the start, when the movement began. Let's suppose that advertising has saturated the verbi-vocal-visual space; this triad constitutes the word on its three fronts: semantic, sonorous, and plastic-visual. And let's suppose that there is again a need for a certain sense of interiority, which hopefully will not take us back to a known place prior to the avant-gardes and to a need to escape again. This interiority does not have to be the shooting for a search for the ethereal, the abstract, or lachrymose. It can be a precise, efficient interiority. This interior space does not have to be the territory of overflowing forms in the finest confessional ways, and, therefore, full of guilt; not in life, and not in poetry. This can be learned from the notion of concreteness, which is learned by concrete poetry.

BIRD

I would also like it if there were no mystery to the bird, but there is; that there were no mystery in song, but there is; and none in flight, but there is. The mystery consists on a fragility, in the strength of that fragility. The world is really big and the bird really small. The bond that both make generates a field of reciprocal hospitality: one is the soundhole, the other the sound. And the other—which happens to be oneself—listens.

WORDS

There are two versions regarding the responsibility of words: one, that they are not innocent; the other, that they are. Both are true, depending on the situation. What's undisputable is the following: words are beautiful for the simple fact of being words, perhaps for being supported by silence. Words are worn out, in meaning, in worth. They are not very useful, except to fulfil a ritual of a working codification. Today words are more useful in a poem than in an exchange of linguistic communication. We had established that the aesthetic phase of words was a refined distillation from the simple use in everyday speech. But language gets worn-out. And perhaps we have to live with that language, contaminated as it is. In this awareness, poetry enters the game with strength. Because, at least there, in the field of the poem, words acquire a different dimension, a dimension that exists simply because it does, for the hell of it, because there is nothing to be understood; and this is good. And not only good, how amazingly wonderful this is! Of course we must redouble our efforts; it has been seen, we are far from the beginning, almost, perhaps, at a reiterated beginning of something that we have seen or heard once before.

[Talk given at the Writers Refuge House in Mexico City as part of the cycle, *Ten Magic Words for a Writer*]

Translated by David Nielsen and Antonio Ochoa

Between Listeners, Loss: A Conversation with Eduardo Milan[1]

In the present conditions—conditions marked by a capitalism that increasingly acts—as you have called it—as a '[levelling] system', what could one possibly expect from poetry? What connection can it offer in the context of a massively hegemonic culture?

We must expect the impossible from poetry: that it unveils ways of transformation. For this reason, it should stop being an alienating practice that alternates between the eternal and the contingent. Poetry is always contingent; or it's not a primary concern. We shouldn't poison ourselves with the eternal. Those are the masters of Poetic Power, which also exists. And it has more followers than we have possibilities to continue talking. Poetry has a considerable quantity of loss. To work with loss is the most difficult thing of all. You must stand before the listeners—listeners are rare, extremely rare—and say: 'poetry is about loss, do you want to lose?' The one that remains, reads you.

Keeping in mind a historic moment in which language is frequently emptied, normalized, and stripped of any dangerousness, what strategies might we encourage in order to recuperate more subversive uses of poetic language, including the register of 'babbling'? What breaches exist for a poetic discourse of resistance?

I believe one must communicate—in the sense of making contact, not of exchanging meanings—through that which isn't necessarily communicable. Communication is 'something more', poetically speaking, but it isn't the meaning of a poem; nor is it a cloister that hides the poem. Today it is more important to leave meaning suspended than to wall it up in a cloister. The

---

[1] This interview forms part of a series of interviews by the poets Laura Giordani, Arturo Borra, and Viktor Gómez with key authors of contemporary Spanish-language poetry.

quality of the hedgehog that Derrida gives poetry is correct. The great worth of poetry lies in its bristles, in its ability to bristle, to bristle on account of its own bristly-ness, not by terrorizing, not by putting one's hairs on end. Communication isn't the problem. This is no longer even the topic. The incommunicable is difficult to manage, it's true; but more than finding ourselves incommunicado, we are desolated. We are powerless before the way the world is heading and in the fact that not everyone is so. This is an ideological-moral transformation of poetry that not everyone endorses because, in principle, poetry has nothing to do with this. It is what drives the 'neutral ones' to rage in their attitude to poetry: they become all about origins, beginnings. They combine the proletariat and monarchy by the magic of rhyme. They become true Humanists, modern Petrarchs. However, poetry is not just any story, and not everyone is a poet. The first thing is to respond with specifics, and then we march. Ours is the word, the relationship with words. Poets are not the only ones, but we give a distinct sense to that use of language. The problem is the exclusion of certain areas of signification that grant meaning. This is what the media-consensual power does. It could be said that we are criminals because we don't agree with its way of using language. Their way of using the language of reality and the reality of language is completely elementary. A problem today is… another problem! This is so tiresome. We don't want any more problems. What do we want? We need to return to a work of poetry as a distinct form of gratification. We need to threaten with the difficult; to do away with the easy alternatives. Bush's famous statement in Iraq: 'They may not have weapons of mass destruction but opportunities may arise.' That's good for murderers, investors, and Directors of Chaos, but not for poetry. We must restrict the alternatives. I'm not talking about any kind of agitation. This is how I understand compromise: choice. The world today is always correctable. If it's not this way, then it's that way, if it isn't Dada, then it's baroque. No, you have to make a choice. Playing things by ear is fine at the start, but then you must choose a path. To work with what is inaccessible in poetry. There is a side that is accessible in poetry. But there's a side that's inaccessible. If you want to play with the Olympic, pre-capitalist logic of win-lose, there you win. The enemy exists. He is going to deny that he is the enemy. The enemy should know that poetry is a way of taking sides, something as responsible as changing the world. It's not a question of maintenance. They conserve this world and we sustain it.

Is there any value anymore in claiming a 'sense of commitment' that isn't just a declaration of good intentions? And what do we even mean when we speak of commitment?

I believe that I answered that already. But to extend the reasoning of the platitude, commitment is the ritual before marriage. Getting married is what happens with poetry. Marriage is a word that does not sound right to me… weddings.

What characteristics do you think set a poetic text apart from other artistic texts (verbal, visual, aural), including those within literary genres such as the novel, biography, or the essay?

I would say that the poetic text charges its main constituent—the word—in a unique way. It is something dense yet ungraspable. That is the first thing, a poem is a paradoxical entity. It is, but it isn't; it's useful but it's not useful; it dies but it doesn't die. It seems like a golden age, but it is one of stone; of fire, air, water, and stone. The poem ends in the air but it begins in the stone. Then, the relations between words are not instrumental; that is to say, they aren't aimed at one type of communication, a way of 'knowing the world.' Poetry uncovers, opens, radiates. A poetic text doesn't have a specific boundary. It can jump to the essay, it can tell its own story or another story, all of this from within. If there is a specificity, it's an awareness of its own materiality, of its material thickness. Of this there cannot be any doubt. It has to be there in order to have its place. All this is in regard to the interior. What specifically plays in the exterior, in a world seized by exteriority? I believe it must displace itself, untie itself, as far as it is possible. The poetic text has something of being persecuted. Not because a crime was committed. The only crime a poem might have committed is to leave behind a place, a homeland, a love, a fountain, or the shadow of a bird of paradise. But we must keep in mind that all of this could come after the poem. Rather because this notion is placed in a position of discomfort, it creates spaces of discomfort in relation to the regulation of space. I don't believe that the poetic text mistrusts *things*; perhaps it mistrusts their names; and yes, without a doubt their positions. Not because things are essentially out of place and the poetic text would regulate those places in an onto-spatial devolution, but because spaces are not innocent. We were born with the spaces occupied. We must talk about the manipulation of the grass. In this sense, I do not believe that the poetic text comes to return anything. If it does it is to redistribute a field of action. And if it doesn't come to do that, it's better that it does not come at all. However, this is not going happen.

What role does your childhood play in your poetic modulation, affected as it was by the political repression promoted by Latin American military dictatorships? In broader terms, what Southern trails—as spaces of articulation—are present in your writing?

I was indelibly marked by the imprisonment of my father. I spent six years coexisting—1973 to 1979—with his prison from outside, going to see him. Later I couldn't take it anymore and went into exile. My father remained in prison for another six years, for the duration of the dictatorship. Total time in prison, twelve years. The personal balance sheet after those twelve years was the cancer that killed him. Post-dictatorial Uruguayan medicine prolonged his life as long as it could; it is very good. My father's imprisonment prolonged my childhood, in the sense that—even though I published right after he entered prison (*Liberty*, that was the name of the prison)—childhood is that 'which doesn't speak.' It's as if that poetry were written but could not speak. This poetic period of my life is very important for me because in disentangling all of this I understand more about writing than I would reading the non-existent literary criticism of the period. To know poetry one must be able to read the smoke signals, not literary criticism. This is the curse that falls on all of us: classes, fateful literature classes. But before this I had been marked by the death of my mother, when I was about to turn two. Southern trails: my mother was Brazilian, my father Uruguayan. Brazil was the first Latin American dictatorship in 1964, and the best Latin American poetry. I straddled the two languages, riding astride a two-tongued horse. I have never lost sight of this. Often I think and hear the sound in Portuguese though I write Spanish. At the end of the day, the fate of my last names had to help me write.[2] What Brazilian music doesn't have is critical awareness. Drums are great, but more drum is the silence that goes from one drumbeat to the next; the pause—not the peace—between drumbeats. Silence is awareness. This awareness was put on the map by Concrete poetry in 1950; and before that, in 1928, with Oswald de Andrade and his 'Cannibal Manifesto,' whence concrete poetry comes—in critical terms of this specific geography. I always knew that my poetic conflict was going to be precisely with this 'place of articulation,' that from the awareness of there being a lack, and later a substitution, a mobility, a border crossing, was going emerge my possibility to write concentrating on, precisely, impossibilities.

The concept of borders is an important one for me. Not only because I was born in the borderlands between Brazil and Uruguay, or because my mother's family name was Damilano and my father's Milán, but because my name means 'guardian of the border.' Inevitably one falls for a personal poetic mythology. This is why I don't like to talk about myself in my writing—not, at least, with the credit that others take for themselves and their tragedies unless the party we throw for ourselves and all the tragic events of our lives includes others and their own tragedies—because the assembled, eventful destiny seems invented, improbable. What is grave seems to turn trivial, a blackmail to win prizes.

---

[2] In Hispanic countries a person's full name is composed of the father's family name and mother's family name, thus Eduardo Milán (father's family name) Damilano (mother's family name).

The trivialization of the experience of love as depicted by the culture industry very often gets in the way of our seeing the profoundly significant position love holds in the human experience. How can we still write love poetry and, even more importantly, how can we rebuild an awareness of love that is different than what has already been thought, already felt, as Mario Perniola warns us?

A human being is a being moved by desire. 'Love' is a word that belongs to the language of Latin American soap operas (and that some on the Left usually use with great profit in Venezuela, Mexico, or Colombia), and to the nineteenth century on the iron benches of town squares in the provinces. Brazilians don't say 'love,' they say 'sex.' They love to follow the lead of their model, the United States. In fact, it was the first Latin American society penetrated by that model and it continues to be one of the strongest ones in its conviction to consume. Their love for their own bodies, whose exterior metaphor is the beach, is proverbial. Brazilians lost their intimacy on the beach under the sun at Ipanema. We—South American para-Hispanics—lost it with the aesthetics of the historical avant-gardes. I mean there are different levels. When the Americans started 'to have sex,'[3] we began not making 'love.' Everybody can do what he or she wants, this is the Great Age of Entitlement. We, I mean, the people of poetry, can't live without love. Dante said it, 'Love moves the sun and other stars.' We—the 'other stars'—are also moved by love. In terms of writing a love poem is, within the uncertain current poetic logic if one wants be coherent with the times, completely unthinkable. A love poem is the unthinkable within the uncertain. A love poem comes out complete, it is the product of an epiphany, and it cannot be argued with. And you don't play with the words in a love poem, unless it's a love poem that doesn't want to be a love poem. That's the kind of poem that saturated the market. There is a poetic impossibility, to transmit conviction of emotion without falling into emotional blackmail. Latin American poetry is the most blackmailing poetry in the world since its discovery, through the colonial period to modern

---
[3] In English in the original

societies and dictatorships. If reality was brutal, the poetry that lamented it was worse. Not everybody is the Inca Garcilaso and Guamán Poma, not everybody is Darío or Carlos Martínez Rivas. It's not that there is too much crying, there is too much lamentation. The teardrop, the crystallized pear that spills from the eye, is the best of love poetry in Latin America because it's very infrequent; or, on the other hand, the cold ironic detachment in Neruda's Poem 'Twenty.' Love is suffering and joy. But the love poem is merely elegance.

Currently there are a few dominant poetry clans that have taken control of publishing outlets and are attempting to colonize the artistic scene. This seems to push other poets to face a dilemma, to either reproduce this clan logic or risk being ostracized. What alternatives are there for poets unwilling to submit to this dilemma? How does one participate in an 'exile in language' without surrendering to silence or forced marginalization?

This is the poetic borderland. Poetry can also be an instance of resistance by pure poetry. That is, poetry not merely as a weapon against the system, by means of poetry by devotion to a practice that exists in the margins. Augusto de Campos used to give the example of the bear, enough honey to suck its own paws during the winter. One must have those reserves. I like what the question suggests because we shouldn't believe for a second that poetry escaped the notion of grouping, whose true name is mafia. Let's look at the Soviet Union. The result of the fall of true-socialism is the proliferation of mafia groups. There is a becoming a sect when there is the death—albeit partial—of courage, of hope. Otherwise there is community, the struggle for the common. This isn't to say that 'poetry should be made by everyone,' but that the world is for everyone. The mentality of the clan, sectarian, or mob, reproduces a dominating mentality—even perhaps a mode of production. The real-poetry groups and the real-publishing groups also create exclusion. That is the hidden name: exclusion, to send the other through the floodgates. With regard to living an exile in language, poetry is the exile of language so long as it remains poetry. Poetic language has no country. The system attempts to transform the value with multiple awards. Afterwards the poet doesn't know what to do with his accounts. He becomes a lover of the pragmatic, 'we should take whatever is possible from the system,' etc. Then he begins to justify everything. But by this point he has long ago abandoned poetry. Something important to remember is that poetry can also be lost; even without ever stop writing it, which is interesting.

How does one ponder the link with the readers that isn't mediated by the logic of branding—by labels more or less profitable, more or less stigmatized—that as the same time it classifies poetics it disregards the individualization of aesthetics?

Whenever one goes to do a reading one must be prepared to teach something about art and aesthetics, politics and ecology, world and underworld. The reader is limited to information. We haven't left Baudelaire yet. The reader doesn't know this. There is an introjected faith in the media's conditioning us to believe that the vulgarization of every day living as opinion has more credibility than a true happening or event. There is a need to be amazed. We need to ask ourselves how and why in times of 'hardship' poetry 'is successful,' it 'moves mountains' ('mountains of people,' obviously, friendly people, captive people), and it resurrects ghosts. There isn't much mystery here. It isn't consciousness, but the need to belong. It is powerlessness in the form of a community. It isn't an awareness of art, but the need for solace. It isn't the need for poetry, but the need to believe in something that can't be verified, that isn't visible (as Antonio Méndez Rubio would say), that doesn't cost—better still, that doesn't have a face. Because the concrete and the tangible, the marketable, what becomes future, that which reaches the end of the month smoothly like a seraphim does not belong to us. A little distrust in the success of poetry doesn't hurt. To stop believing in the winning poets and their agonizing awards is essential. If we don't get off the train of triumphalism that implies a mutual congratulating because suffering poets are blessed by success, then we will never realize that the system operates not with the poets but through them. Poetry is for maintaining dignity, not for winning, and not for starving to death either. We should ask the poet, the artist, for what is ethical. Zitarrosa[4] used to tell me: 'I try not to write a single word I can't claim responsibility for.' This isn't just anything. Because he wasn't thinking only of 'long live the proletariat!' or 'down with the dictator!' (Back then there actually were proletariat and dictators; today we have bullies, the bullied, and those who want to climb the pecking order). It's a difficult line. But it is a fundamental ethics that is demanded there. Poets, artists, they are the ones who betray, not the public. The great play of administration of the system's existence consists in regulating the taste of the receptor, of the reader, making him believe that he's defining something. But he doesn't define anything; a captive cannot define anything. Poets define, artists betray.

Keeping in mind the indefinable condition of poetry—or at least the persistent failures to capture its characteristics in some kind of specific formula—what would you say isn't poetry? Is there a place, a crossing, at which point poetry begins to dissolve?

I'll try a positive construction, to define it by what it is. Poetry, in the sense that I like, is the act of an extreme non-existent that accepts becoming possible. Although it never forgets its fundamental essence: that which makes sounds. That is what the troubadours called, precisely, *trobar*, the unnecessary remembered. Poetry is unforgettable. Its invisibility is forever putting it to the test. Hunger, humiliation, the degradation of others, they all leave their mark, their footprint. Hypothetically they could disappear. We don't want that to happen, but they aren't creations.

In your essays you make multiple references to the legacies of the avant-gardes, especially the Latin American avant-gardes. You say

---

[4] Alfredo Zitarrosa (Uruguay, 1936-1989), poet, singer-songwriter.

that this legacy is more than simply form, and that its implications are political, philosophical, that they have to do with a way of life. Even so, after these aesthetic experiences, is there room left for formal experimentation? Are there any real possibilities for variation for the neo-avant-garde to pursue that would end up being more than simply exercises in repetition?

The avant-garde has to do with two things, the forms art takes and an attitude towards art and the world. The usual attitude of the West towards the avant-garde is of a story of 'bad moment' for art that has happily come and gone. What remains is form acting as form, art object acting as art object, both harmless. Well, nice story! We've had this story for nearly a century. It is prevalent but it is false. The numbness in contemporary art, the 'ethical' daydreaming of contemporary art—the 'good things of an evil world' accepted by capital, by the governments that hate democracy but speak on its behalf, this great desolate confusion that we suffer as evidence of our collapse that refuses to understand, what is there to understand—cannot be explained culturally but rather as a kind of visceral and ideological rejection both to the dissolving spirit of the historical avant-garde—the horror of an era of living without art, the modern era, that can only explain itself through art—and the avant-garde's problematic, discontinuous, explosive, and disturbing attitude in comparison to mainstream society. Contemporary art carried out a successful counter-strike against the avant-garde capitalizing its formal resources. What contemporary art can't capitalize on is its attitude. The avant-garde's attitude is consubstantial to all forming and transforming art practice. This is the reason why the avant-garde cannot disappear. The fanatic ecumenical voice that claims to speak on behalf of 'the people,' on behalf of 'us,' and thanks both God and Tradition for the disappearance of the avant-garde, has no idea what he's talking about. The art that is made and that will be made after the avant-garde has the avant-garde inside it, or it has a hole with an arrow signalling its absence. I'm thinking particularly of the traditionalism of the Homeland, Family, and Fixed Form that claims to speak on behalf of humanity. The forms of the avant-garde—the legacy of a repertoire of its forms—without the avant-garde's attitude to support and inspire them, are cold, trivial, snobbish, and elitist. Furthermore, these would be stupid, with that vindictive attitude of the *nouveau riche*, to whom at long last *destiny*—or perhaps corruption—has brought justice. But how, if the end—albeit without end, Kantianly speaking—is the ideological foundation of the tastes of the bourgeoisie, consumer of art! We are moving, imperceptibly, from the threat of the horror of being without art to the threat of the horror of being without water slowly, with concern. You can't make art reserves. You can't put away thirst. It never passes through our minds that what one can really do without is horror.

At various moments in your essays you question a 'poetry of the possible' that ends in what you call 'now-ness', a focus that loses sight of any political alternatives. Are you suggesting, then, the promise of a 'poetry of the impossible'? And this poetry, might we think of it as a kind of 'utopianism' in contrast to the 'poetry of the possible' that you describe?

Now-ness is, of course, the inability to leave the present moment. It is the claustrophobia of the present. It's like being in a cage. Poetry is a cage, certainly. But the poem opens the door. Whether the birds fly away or stay inside is not the responsibility of the poet. More than likely they will fly away. But 'now' isn't a constraint, a limitation; rather it's a part of the clock. One lives now, tomorrow, and the next day. Poetry will always be written 'now,' but not *for* 'the now.' If it is, then it means that we are surrounded. 'Now-ness' is capitalism. It is a frenzy for 'now,' no thought for tomorrow, for what will remain. One must live now the same as before or after. It's the poetic life to throw 'now' into disarray, to dislocate it, to place it farther away. This system of the great revelation, where everything shows itself in order to control you better, is like something out of Bataille, but positive; he dilapidated the system, he resisted accumulation. There exists, on the other hand, the dominant dilapidation of capital in the form of plundering, in the depletion of resources. The capitalistic system doesn't look to the future because it believes in conversion: the water runs out and it becomes a reptile. There is always an option. One must have the resources to exercise it. We must tell them what a terrible illusion this is. Illusion is good. The poet knows that. It is the best of us. Idiot, idler, dreamer are true synonyms applicable to the poet. But capitalism lives the illusion without any real confidence. It only believes in the present because it has identified the present with seeing. The end exists. Whoever denies the future denies the end and vice versa. Utopia is still there. You can make it invisible. But it's still there.

You suggested in your book Resistir *that 'to write today is still to mourn the death of the creator.' This sentence seems to resonate with a certain French philosophical tradition—where we find Barthes or Foucault—that has talked on numerous occasions about the 'death of the subject.' Do you think that the thesis of a 'writing without a subject' is a valid way of discussing poetic writing, or does it refer more to a specific mode of talking about the subject? More generally, what are the connections you would identify between poetry and the subject?*

'To mourn the death of the creator' is precisely that, to see your self from the outside. The action of verse is to move outward. To cry is shed tears outside. What I don't go along with is the idea of a univocal identity. To write is to access a plurivocal identity, an ugly word. It is from the outside in a lack of place in relation to this identity with which one lives, to write oneself to the outside; if we want to call another real, good. Governments—media capitalists—are the owners of the meanings of words in their usual, everyday sense. We mustn't forget this. Meaning is granted from there, not from poetry, not from dictionaries, not from the deposits of meaning—I don't know where these are, where memory has remained intact. But I detest the intact, what remains intact, the nun-virginal universe. To keep us calm they dress memory up in this habit, and they do the same to poetry. Not Steiner nor Foucault nor Bataille nor Blanchot but the poets, the Latin American poets, the French poets that fled Commune, the poets of the old This-Regime that fled what they betrayed as of the plague towards the abyss of capitalism. They end in pornography like Russian girls. What horror is that? No, I don't believe in the death of the subject where Cartesianism ends up like a *Cartesianism*. We have to stop killing, in the sense of that generic, widespread slaughter. Otherwise we'll never be able to live this place. We must save life, educate how to save lives. I think the negative application to art and thought is correct. But speaking dialectically it isn't possible to live in a negative key. What we find in those deaths of the subject is a stance that is fundamentally anti-dialectic. It's not the Foucault that I love. I love the one who, precisely, identifies Power. 'Subject,' more than a concept, is an exceptionally dangerous word. In its name is written a destination. In order to see it, you must move outward. And with the word there one must make it subjective in order to no longer being subjected. The sense of apprehension that is the tragic sense of the hero's relation to God must be brought to justice, to make it just. Otherwise we remain in a dependent relationship with the gods or substitutes who don't care about us. Power doesn't care about us, that's why it submits us. It's not that it wants us in order to submit us. For me, things are even worse than they seem. Those corporate powers that devour your body don't care about you; or they want you devoured by corporate power. Corporations are body eaters. The Myth of the Great Body, the body remade by the Mythical Father is the sum of all the devoured bodies of his children, nephews, etc. That is why Tupac Amaru's body is still floating in pieces. And all of the relatives that make up Big Brother's great family—this is, without a doubt, the great betrayal of all fraternity, as long as this brother, that incest, remains the figure that can be desecrated, to violate, camera in hand, our most intimate moments, to humiliate (which is something more difficult with the Father). These are a series of lying metaphors—although the use of brother is metonymical, of course. Metaphor is not an innocent trope. Metaphor is the great trope of complicity because it leaves whenever it's convenient; the reading by syllables letting the words decompose. That's when the bodies really begin to get eaten up. Poetry must denounce this. Poetry cannot be complicit to the assassination—the suicide—of metaphor when it gives way to literality. It's what has happened with the poetry that has accepted back the re-composition of the 'metaphorical body,' as if nothing had ever happened. We accept, nothing has happened here. But then, whose footprints are those? Marcos tried it with the prefix *sub*. It doesn't have anything to do with being beneath—he, in his case, beneath the Command of Indigenous Peoples—this makes sense. But when one is not dependent upon a people or with a people behind to whom one must give account, I consider it unfortunate, this cheering for the descent of the 'I,' of my self, which is, in short, the story of the impossibility of being. It's about the ability to be, not abandonment, not forgetting, the two great nihilistic and post-nihilistic sufferings. It's about making the impossible possible.

Translated by David Nielsen

www.ingramcontent.com/pod-product-compliance
Lightning Source LLC
Chambersburg PA
CBHW031157160426
43193CB00008B/409